"As youth culture continues to change at breakneck speed, I meet a growing number of youth workers and parents who feel more and more out of touch and intimidated by kids. Let's face it: Taking that first step to build a relationship with a kid is intimidating. I'm grateful for Jonathan McKee and his ability to show us how to get past our fears to connect with relationships that are real and deep. *Connect* is a valuable and encouraging tool that not only helps us take that crucial first step, but also it helps us to keep walking further and further so that we might lead kids deeper and deeper into the faith."

—Dr. Walt Mueller, president, Center for Parent/Youth Understanding; author, *Youth Culture 101*

"In a youth ministry world full of 'the next new thing,' it's easy to get sidetracked from Jesus' Great Commandment and Great Commission. Jonathan McKee calls us back to these core essentials in *Connect*, providing a practical, powerful, hands-on strategy for connecting with teens one-on-one. By purposefully pursuing deeper spiritual conversations, Jonathan shows us how loving students and sharing the message of the gospel will unleash God's transforming power and change lives forever. *Connect* challenges us to honestly assess where our teens are spiritually and provides the focus, insight, and practical tips we need to significantly impact the life of every teen we encounter."

—Greg Stier, president, Dare 2 Share Ministries; author, *Venti Jesus Please* and *Dare 2 Share: A Field Guide to Sharing Your Faith*

"This is what healthy youth ministry is all about. Jonathan McKee has developed a great paradigm for reaching students and moving them toward becoming lifelong disciples."

—Jim Burns, Ph.D., president, HomeWord; author, *Confident Parenting*, *The Purity Code*, and *Creating an Intimate Marriage*

"It seems to me that God is all about relationships. So much so that he broke into our world to let us get to know him. Jonathan has come up with the ultimate book on relationships. This maybe the most important topic he has written about. *How do you connect with the diversity of students where you live? How do you get them to connect with each other? How do you get them to connect with God?* Jonathan gives practical answers to these questions and more. *Connect* is filled with helpful stories of real kids and genuine youth workers. It's an easy-to-follow book with realistic steps you can use to take your youth ministry to the next level. I belive chapter fourteen alone may be worth the price of the book because it reveals how little we know about our students; Jonathan then offers a series of questions to remedy the situation. I've seen Jonathan do this with my university students in my classes and have watched the light go on above their heads. They suddenly get it, and their ministries are transformed."

—Les Christie, chair, youth ministry department, William Jessup University; author, *When Church Kids Go Bad*

"*Connect* needs to be in the hands of everyone—paid or unpaid— who works with kids for the cause of Christ. It's so easy to read and so full of practical tips and stories that it succeeds in becoming the kind of rare book that both inspires and instructs, a standalone coaching resource I urge our YFC family to use with all of our adult volunteers. By drilling deeply into one of youth ministry's most significant pressure points, I hope that Jonathan will lead readers to 'tap out' and surrender to the challenge of making one-on-one relationships with every type of young person their priority."

—Dr. Dave Rahn, Youth for Christ/USA Chief Ministry Officer and Huntington University Director of MA in Youth Ministry Leadership (www.youthministryleadership.com)

"*Connect* is on point! Once you read it you'll be encouraged to continue the journey of loving kids in an isolated world. Jonathan has captured a timely truth on these pages that the church is desperately in need of today."

—Fred Lynch, founder, GodStyle Productions; author, *The Script*

"There are a lot of books out there that talk about the importance of relationships in regard to youth community, discipleship, and evangelism. This by far is the most practical book I've ever read that actually moves the discussion further to actually implementing a strategy and structure to make it happen."

—Dan Kimball, author, *They Like Jesus but Not the Church*

"This is the way to 'do' all youth ministry. In a very succinct manner Jonathan has positioned *Connect* to help lead people to a deeper understanding of the difference between a programmatic approach and a relational ministry with teenagers. I'm a Young Life guy, and Jonathan has more accurately and articulately described our ministry than some of our own training materials. I applaud Jonathan's push to get people out of the youth room and into the world of teenagers. This book helps all of us continue on the quest to value and actually implement a more Jesus-style of ministry with young people today...thank you!"

—Dan Jessup, director of leadership development, Africa, Asia, and Latin America, Young Life

REAL RELATIONSHIPS IN A WORLD OF ISOLATION

CONNECT

JONATHAN MCKEE

ZONDERVAN®

ZONDERVAN.com/
AUTHORTRACKER
follow your favorite authors

youth
specialties

YOUTH SPECIALTIES

Connect: Real Relationships in a World of Isolation
Copyright 2009 by Jonathan McKee

Youth Specialties resources, 1890 Cordell Ct. Ste. 105, El Cajon, CA 92020 are published by Zondervan, 5300 Patterson Ave. SE, Grand Rapids, MI 49530.

Library of Congress Cataloging-in-Publication Data

McKee, Jonathan R. (Jonathan Ray), 1970-
    Connect : real relationships in a world of isolation / by Jonathan McKee.
      p. cm.
    Includes bibliographical references.
    ISBN 978-0-310-28777-3
    1. Church work with teenagers. 2. Interpersonal relations—Religious
aspects—Christianity. I. Title.
BV4447.M2365 2009
259'.23—dc22   2009033742

Cover design by SharpSeven Design
Interior design by Mark Novelli, IMAGO

Printed in the United States of America

---

10 11 12 13 14 15 • 20 19 18 17 16 15 14 13 12 11 10 9 8 7 6 5 4 3

CONTENTS

SHOUT OUTS

Life with God is all about relationships.

God is relationship driven. I am so thankful to God for his relationship with me and the relationships he has put in my life. God is the reason behind this book. God came down to earth to connect with me personally, and he wants me to connect with others.

A huge thanks to my family: Lori, Alec, Alyssa, and Ashley. They always know when a book is due...and they probably don't enjoy me very much the last few weeks before a deadline. Thanks for putting up with me. You're my favorites!

I also have to send a special shout out to a group of people that has helped me with several books now. These people have read several versions of these manuscripts, marked them up, given me positive and negative feedback, and helped me with the final tweaks. This group is made up of my family: My Dad, my wife Lori, and my brother Thom; my coworkers: David, Todd, and Danette; and my youth ministry buddies: KJ, Furb, Brandon, and Andy. Thanks for your different perspectives and for helping me communicate to a variety of audiences.

Much love to the other youth workers in the field whose stories I used in this book: Tonya, Trazy, John, PJ, Josh, Aaron, Susan, Graham, and Wendy.

Special thanks to Roni and Jay, the YS crew that makes it happen. You guys rock!

Peace! Love! Mercy!

Jonathan McKee

CONNECTING THROUGH REAL RELATIONSHIPS

1
THE IMPACT OF ONE-ON-ONE

Last month a student from the high school just down the street from me excused himself from class about 10:15 a.m., walked into a restroom, and shot himself.

It was his 17th birthday.

My heart sank as I read the entire story in our local Sacramento paper. That's the third article this week I've seen about teenage anxiety, depression, violence, and self-injury. Anyone in contact with youth notices their stress, pain, and emptiness.

As youth workers, we read books to try to understand a youth culture that seems to be growing more relationally disconnected and distant. Book titles like *Hurt*[i] and *Helping Teenagers in Crisis*[ii] are becoming more commonplace. Young people are in pain, and they are seeking others who can identify with those feelings.

Ironically, this generation that feels so alone is looking for comradery in the wrong place...seclusion. The Friday night hangout is drifting away from a physical place with living, breathing bodies. Alone, in the privacy of their own bedrooms, kids flock to virtual hangouts and encircle themselves with e-friends—surrounded, yet isolated.

Technology allows young people to instantly connect to others digitally while staying geographically isolated from them. Their favorite social networking site brags several hundred friends—yet somehow they still feel alone. The tools supposed to cultivate connection leave students wanting more—and for good reason. E-friends can't fill the tangible, relational void in students' lives.

Whether realized or not, all of us long for face-to-face relationships.

We need them.

Recently, artist Evan Baden created a series of photographs called *The Illuminati*, depicting current children and teenagers in a common light–the glow of their electronic devices on their faces. Baden's words describing the photographs are almost more revealing than the pictures themselves:

> From our earliest memories, there has always been a way to connect with others, whether it is MySpace, Facebook, cell phones, e-mail, or instant messenger. And now, with the Internet, instant messaging, and e-mail in our pocket, right there with our phones, we can always feel as if we are part of a greater whole. These devices grace us with the ability to instantly connect to others, and at the same time, they isolate us from those with whom we are connected.[iii]

Considering the increase in time spent communicating, one might assume technology helps young people build deeper relationships. However, statistics show us quite the opposite. Students and young adults have fewer close friends than their peers of just a decade ago.[iv] I believe the lack of face-to-face time is dissolving relationships, and wounds from this are beginning to emerge in the lives of teens all around us.

As I write this chapter, I'm traveling on a plane that just left Chicago. During takeoff I picked up the airline's magazine. Flipping through the magazine I noticed an advertisement for a dating service. It read:

> With over 100 million unattached people in the U.S., why is it so difficult for singles to meet? In an age where the BlackBerry is a true companion, and people have become so fixated on their real-time/anytime correspondence, has everyone forgotten the simplicity of communicating face-to-face?[v]

The need for face-to-face relationships is becoming so readily apparent that even advertising targets this felt need.

Studies are also showing youth and young adults are participating less in team sports and more in individual activities:

- Since 1998, the number of young adults participating in team sports has decreased from 19 percent to 13 percent.

- The number of young adults going out to the movies has decreased from 13 percent in 1998 to just 3 percent in 2008.

- The number of adolescents staying home to watch television or rent videos has increased from 24 percent in 1998 to 32 percent in 2008.[vi]

It seems to me students today are more isolated, have fewer close friends, and are drifting away from activities with personal interaction. This is creating a relational void in their lives. Add this to the growing levels of stress and pain teenagers already face as part of adolescence, and it is no wonder we are seeing an increase in teenage anxiety, depression, violence, and self-injury. Teenagers are hurting more than ever before.

Where is the hope? How can we make an impact in the lives of today's lonely and hurting teenagers? Is there anything a caring adult can do?

Is it possible the solution might be somewhere beyond technology's reach? Could the answer be found in something as simple as a *face-to-face* meeting and good, old-fashioned, one-on-one interaction?

JARED

Jared seemed impossible to reach. Students warned me about him the first time he walked in the door of our weekly youth group meeting. He seemed polite enough when I met him, but it didn't take long for him to live up to his reputation. Whenever I talked— Jared was talking. Whenever there was a problem in one of our small groups—it was Jared's small group. If there was a disturbance in the Taco Bell parking lot after youth group, my first question was always, "Where's Jared?"

But something miraculous happened one day. I took Jared out for a soda, and Jared and I sat face-to-face, eating, laughing, and talking. For the first time ever, Jared looked into my eyes and shared his home life with me. We connected.

He wasn't distracted by his friends or preoccupied with impressing the girls around him. I took time to listen to Jared, and then, Jared began listening to me. I slowed down enough to meet with him *one-on-one*.

KERI

Keri was a student leader in our senior high group. She'd accepted Christ in early adolescence and was growing in her faith each year. By her junior year she was put in charge of our Easter break mission trip. Her senior year she led a Bible study and was probably more reliable than many of our adult volunteers. But Keri was looking for something more than she was receiving from youth group, small groups, and Sunday morning. Keri wanted a mentor—she wanted to be discipled.

Keri started meeting with Cindi weekly at a booth in the corner of a little restaurant by her house. Cindi was a caring adult from our church who had connected with Keri. She wasn't technically part of our volunteer staff, but she made herself available to disciple a few girls at different times during the week. They read a chapter of a book each week and discussed it together over a chocolate shake.

Of all the activities, events, and memories Keri experienced in high school, she looks back on her weekly time with Cindi as her most valuable time. Someone cared for her enough to meet with her *one-one-one*.

MONICA

Monica had never been taught to take care of herself. With an absent dad and a full-time working mom, Monica had been left to raise herself and her brother on microwave dinners. Her breath was foul and her social skills were poor. Even my adult volunteers steered clear of her, not out of a lack of compassion but a lack of understanding of how to handle her. Monica was very difficult.

Monica wasn't a popular student. Whenever she entered the junior high room at our church, you could sense the other students thinking, "Great, there goes the evening."

But then Gina game along. Gina was one of my volunteers who had a rough history of her own. She understood what it was like being raised by a single mom who worked full time and the weight of the responsibility of caring for a younger brother.

Gina began hanging out with Monica and began understanding her like none of my other leaders could. At first she'd just pick her up and take her home from youth group. But that grew to fast-food stops and even overnighters during which the two would stay up watching old movies, stuffing their faces with popcorn. Gina connected with Monica like no one else ever had.

In just six months Monica became a different person. She grew more comfortable with who she was in God's eyes, gained confidence, and become more social. She began to care about the way she dressed and took care of herself in other ways. She developed better personal hygiene. But the biggest difference we noticed in Monica was the smile she wore all the time.

She had a reason to smile. Someone had taken the time to notice her. Someone was willing to give her a gift she'd never received—personal time. Monica felt loved for the first time in her life because someone was willing to spend time with her *one-on-one*.

BRIAN

I'll never forget when Brian prayed to receive Christ. We were in a local fast-food joint at about four o'clock on a sunny March afternoon. He had been coming to our campus outreach for about nine months already and had heard me share the gospel multiple times. He always seemed responsive to what we were saying, nodding on cue, even answering our questions with insight. Brian seemed like he was getting a lot out of our discussions. But he never gave any indication he wanted to make a life change—until that day in the restaurant.

Back in October I'd asked Brian if he wanted to grab some nachos after school sometime, and he quickly accepted my invitation. I met his dad as he picked Brian up from our outreach club and asked his permission. His dad was happy I wanted to spend time with his son. So Brian and I hung out at least once a month. We'd connect by either grabbing nachos, video gaming at a mini-golf arcade, or playing Frisbee golf. (We were the only two on the course without mullets.) Sometimes Brian would even join our family for dinner.

Then that March afternoon in our normal booth at a local restaurant, Brian asked me about my job and why I decided to become a youth pastor. I told him about how much I cared for students like him, and how I wanted to see them succeed. Brian nodded appropriately as he scooped the last puddle of cheese from the bottom of the nachos container. Feeling a nudge from God, I asked Brian a pointed question, "Why do *you* think I do all this?"

Brian stopped his chewing and gave me the articulate answer I expected: A shrug of the shoulders accompanied by the grunt commonly accepted as "I don't know," but more specifically verbalized as, "Uh-nu-nuh?"

So I told him. I told him that everything—everything we talked about at youth group, every activity, every fast-food meal—I did was because of God's love for us and God's desire for a relationship with us. Brian nodded on cue just like at youth group. But this time I laid it out right on the table, just the two of us. I shared the gospel with him. I told him the story of God's love for us, despite our sin, and about the sacrifice Christ made on the cross. I asked Brian questions all along, confirming understanding, and finally asking him, "Would you like this relationship with God?" Brian prayed right there in the booth, trusting Jesus with his future—all I did was take time to share with him *one-on-one*.

KRISTEN

One night, Kristen joined our family for dinner. Later in the evening,my wife and I shared the gospel with her, and she eagerly prayed to trust Jesus. When we gave her a Bible, she asked for the page numbers of the verses we had discussed because she didn't know where to find them.

Then we asked her about going to church. Uh-oh! Kristen seemed pretty hesitant. Noticing her uncertainty, we asked what was wrong. She candidly told us, "I've been to church. Church sucks." But when Lori asked Kristen if she could start meeting with her at the house each week and going through the Bible, Kristen said (and I quote), "Hell yeah!" Kristen was interested in God, just not church.

Lori started connecting with Kristen each week. They looked through some foundational passages about God's commitment to us, prayer, worship, church, and fellowship. As Lori and Kristen spent more time talking, studying, and praying, Kristen became more interested in church. But it took baby steps—it took time.

And the only reason she began to change is because Lori discipled her *one-on-one*.

THE COMMON DENOMINATOR

Jared, Keri, Monica, Brian, and Kristen—these students have little in common outside of owning a cell phone and a Facebook page. They may not have even liked each other.

Some were believers when we met them, and some were far from it. Some were curious about God; some didn't think God had a thing to offer. But each was changed by God and eventually plugged into a church home to continue to grow in faith.

The common denominator? Adults who spent time with them *one-on-one*.

Face-to-face conversations can be transformative. It's amazing how God uses one-on-one interaction to shape lives.

I lead an organization called The Source for Youth Ministry. Our Web site has a question-and-answer section called Ask the Source. Each week I receive a huge number of questions from youth workers around the world asking about youth ministry problems, issues, and needs. As the number of these questions increased week to week, I quickly discovered something: *Most of these questions share the same answer.*

As different as many of the questions are, one answer keeps floating to the top. Whether the question is about a problem student, a staff person needing encouragement, a student leader wanting discipleship, or a student with problems getting connected—the answer I provide most often includes *spend time with them one-on-one*.

Sometimes the questions stump me, though. Often when I don't know where to turn, I joke with my coworkers, "When in doubt answer, *spend time with them one-on-one.* It usually works."

MAKING A DIFFERENCE

Relationships are powerful. Without question, the entire Bible is really about relationships: Our relationship with God and our relationship with others. Are you getting to know the students in your ministry area? Do you know their names and their stories?

Do you have a high-maintenance student like Jared in your ministry? Do you know a student like Keri who is showing a lot of promise? How about a student like Monica who just needs to be loved? What about a student like Brian who needs the gospel but never seems to respond in the typical youth group or small group setting? Do you know someone like Kristen—a student who would really love Jesus but isn't too fond of the church right now?

How do you make a difference in the lives of these students? Don't underestimate the impact of *one-on-one*—making a difference *one teen at a time.*

Okay, so maybe you already know *one-on-one* time with teenagers is time well spent, and most likely the problem is more about *how to initiate contact with teens* and *what to say or do* during these one-on-one times. Is there a typical format to these types of face-to-face conversations? Or should we just talk and hang out?

Do we treat a student like Jared different than a student like Brian or Keri? After all, some students are more ready to talk about spiritual things where others seem resistant. How do we talk to these different types of students? Are there any questions or ready-made helps for these situations?

Some of us might be wondering how technology comes into play in our interaction with students. Should we avoid it or use it?

Wow, that's a lot of questions.

In the pages that follow I'll answer each of these questions and provide ideas that will help equip you to talk with six different types of students.

But first let's take a look at how a team of caring adults can make a huge difference if it's willing to prioritize *one-on-one* relationships. Let's take a look at what *one-on-one* is like when in a youth ministry setting.

2

PRIORITY ONE IN YOUTH MINISTRY

Jesse walked into the fast-food joint across the street from the school and quickly found the rest of the adult volunteers huddled in two of the corner booths. Jesse, like the rest of his fellow youth ministry volunteers, reserved five hours a week for hanging out with students. It was Tuesday night, and they'd just finished their weekly youth group meeting—74 students, eight volunteers, one overworked youth pastor named Jay, and only two minor injuries during game time.

After some prayer, Jay asked everyone to talk about how their time with students was going.

While Jesse pondered the question, Kristi, the twentysomething grad student sitting in the booth to his left, spoke up. "Jessica is really opening up," she shared eagerly while dipping a chip in cheese sauce. "I think the discussion on fathers really hit home for her. I'm going to connect with her this weekend for a milkshake and talk with her more about it."

"Trevor liked the talk, too," added Jason, an undergrad student who had volunteered for two years now. Trevor was a student whom Jason had really become close to in the last year. "From my time with Trevor I am sensing he finally might be interested in something more than just basketball and girls."

"Nice," Jay affirmed.

Jesse thought about his time with TJ. He had been a handful since day one but had responded well to Jesse's attention. Jesse always managed to be on TJ's team during games and made sure he was in his small group. Last weekend Jesse had him over to his house to work on his car. Greasy hands and pizza opened up doors to conversation with TJ that Jesse never expected.

Youth group activities are great, small-group sharing is very valuable, but nothing opens doors like one-on-one time with students. In a world where the only words students like TJ usually hear from adults are, "Did you finish your homework?" or, "You're 15 minutes late," or, "Hey, you can't skateboard here," the positive attention TJ received from an affirming adult was making a huge impact.

Jay built his ministry on a foundation of caring adult volunteers who inject themselves into students' lives. Each volunteer commits to Tuesday nights, weekly staff meetings, and quarterly staff training times. But their most important commitment is to "milkshake" conversations by inviting students for dinner or taking them to football games.

This is just a glimpse of what making one-on-one a priority looks like in youth ministry—adults devoting one-on-one time with students, making a difference for Christ, one student at a time.

"ONE THING"

Months ago my friend Brandon, a youth pastor of a growing new church near Sacramento, asked me, "Jonathan, what's the one thing I really need to teach my volunteers this fall?"

Wow! *One thing?* That really narrows it down.

He must have seen the smoke coming out of my ears as my mental gears were grinding to find a simple answer to his question. So he elaborated. "You know, I've got some new volunteers and some who began volunteering last year. What is the most important thing they need to know as we begin our ministry with students this year?"

Good question. How would you answer? The quick reply I gave him was, "Equip your staff to love students and connect with them." But Brandon's question continued to nag at me. *I wondered, Is the answer really that simple? Did other youth workers agree?*

So I set out to research an article on the topic. I surveyed youth workers who use our Web site as a resource, and I talked to a number of authors and youth ministry professors. When I asked them Brandon's question, I was surprised at the similarity of all their responses. The importance of connecting *one-on-one* kept rising to the top.

Saddleback's Kurt Johnston responded quickly with his "priority one" for volunteers: "It's all about relationships."

That sums it up well. It doesn't matter what you call it: Contacting, connecting, building relationships—it's all about our relationships with students. I don't think I received a single response that didn't include this important element. We need to connect with students.

But sometimes this doesn't come naturally. "Connecting can be extremely scary for volunteers at first," shared Don Talley, Senior Director of YFC USA Ministry. "In my experience, volunteers (whether in a church or parachurch ministry) initially struggle with the concept of contacting or initiating relationships with students. Teaching your volunteers the importance of how to initiate a relationship with a teenager can produce a ministry of hospitality and warmth."

Let me ask you this: Do you want uninvolved *chaperones*, or would you rather be part of a youth ministry team that is interacting with students, hanging out with them outside of youth group, and loving them for who they are?

There's a big difference between a youth ministry with what I call *chaperones* and one with volunteers who connect. You may have witnessed a youth ministry that uses chaperones and observed a bunch of students in the middle of the room with the adults around the perimeter in a large horseshoe shape. Guess what? We don't need uninvolved chaperones who want to sit around and talk with each other. Instead we need people who love students and want to get to know them. We need adults who will break out of the horseshoe and start initiating contact with students.

Here's another thought: What if it's not that our adult youth workers don't believe in initiating contact—perhaps they just don't know how?

Youth Specialties President Mark Oestreicher agreed, "I think all volunteers need basic training on how to connect with teenagers."

So how can we help our volunteers not only understand the importance of initiating contact but equip them to do it?

BE LIKE FLATULENCE

I trained my junior high staff how to avoid the "horseshoe" by telling them, "Be like flatulence."

Uh, come again?

Let me explain. Remember in elementary school when everyone sat at their desks quietly working on their math, and the student in the corner of the classroom let out one of those silent-but-deadly ones? One by one, the stench reached each student in the classroom, starting in the corner, working its way to the uttermost parts of the room. If you could watch students respond from above, you would notice students react one by one, the closest first, then finally the farthest away.

This process is called dynamic equilibrium. I can still remember my science teacher Mr. Jenson explaining it to us. He opened a jar of some stinky chemical in one corner of the room and told us to raise our hands when we smelled it. One by one I saw dynamic equilibrium taking place. The molecules spread throughout the entire room until they could spread no more. Hmmmm. Wouldn't that be nice? Wouldn't we all love to see our volunteers spread evenly throughout the room and mixed in with the crowd of students?

At the beginning of each school year, I always invested time in training my staff and volunteers. At these trainings I emphasized that I didn't need uninvolved chaperones; I needed relational staff. I explained the idea of dynamic equilibrium and instructed them to be like molecules seeking dynamic equilibrium. In other words, I wanted to look across the room at any time and see a sea of students with staff members spread throughout—not in bunches, but mixed throughout the students.

My staff never forget the flatulence analogy—crude but effective. Simply dissipate through the room evenly. Whenever I saw staff bunched up in clumps, I simply told them, "Break wind," and they knew exactly what I was talking about.

I've used that analogy for years now in articles and various training seminars. At a recent National Youth Workers Conference, a group saw me and pulled me aside. With a smirk on his face, the leader pulled out a small card they gave to all volunteers which simply read F.A.R.T.—the acronym was even surrounded by artwork of a stench cloud: *Float Around the Room and Talk.* My friend Danette has adopted this acronym and actually puts the word F.A.R.T. on her youth group schedule each night at 6:30 p.m. as a reminder of what her volunteers should be doing.

> Side note: Our adult leaders love connecting with each other as leaders, too. But sometimes you may notice it's difficult to get the leaders to stop mingling with each other and start mingling with students instead. How can you prevent this?

The answer isn't prevention. Rather we need to provide an outlet away from youth group time for leaders to connect with each other.

I've seen numerous youth groups in which adult volunteers were never given the opportunity to mingle and bond with each other as leaders. This isn't good. As a result, it was always much harder to break up staff clumps because they genuinely wanted to see each other and never were given time to connect for even a few minutes. Let's be honest: It's natural to want to say, "Hi," and catch up with your co-volunteers. And it's frustrating when some intense youth pastor breaks up your conversation like a disgruntled algebra teacher. Avoid this problem by creating time for volunteers to hang out together before or after youth group or at your weekly staff meeting. Be proactive by letting them know, "This is the time to connect with each other because we really need to save our youth group time for the students."

MAKING CONNECTING PRIORITY ONE

Encouraging and equipping our volunteers to mingle with students is a great start, but making connecting a priority throughout our entire ministries is a whole different animal. For many of us, *contacting students* is just one little item on our list of training tools—it fits neatly into our Saturday training between *small groups* and *youth culture*. But what would it look like if instead it was at the forefront of what we do?

It's no secret—when I recruited volunteers, I was very clear about their number-one objective: *Spending time with students.* Connecting with students is more important than any programming or logistical need. I wanted my volunteers engaging with students one-on-one.

Think about this: If our volunteers are recruited with the understanding that their number-one job is loving students and hanging out with them, what impact would that have on our youth ministry?

What if we created an atmosphere where every student in your ministry has at least one adult who is crazy about them?

"In order for students to make it, they need dedicated fans," said Brock Morgan, YS workshop presenter, "adults who will come alongside them and walk this journey of life with them—through the good, bad, and the ugly."

"This is NOT something our volunteers JUST do during youth group," added Susan Eaton, a youth worker in northern Kentucky. "I want them emailing students, sending them cards, making some kind of contact with them during the week. Don't just depend on Sunday night (youth group night) to be enough. Be intentional about connecting with them during the week."

Remember Jay, the youth pastor I describe at the beginning of this chapter? His youth ministry volunteers meet every week and report who they are hanging out with and what's going on in their lives. This inventory of changed lives is far more important than any numbers or programming. Jay is all about getting his leaders connected with students.

And hopefully Jay isn't just telling his leaders to do this. A good leader will teach this by example, connecting with students as well.

More than a decade ago I led a junior high ministry. Like Jay, I gathered my adult leaders after youth group so we could share our experiences with students that week. This accomplished two things: 1. It was encouraging to hear how God was working in the lives of students. 2. It kept us accountable—we knew we would be sharing about the time we invested—or didn't invest—with students that week.

I didn't just facilitate these meetings; I took part in them, sharing about my one-on-one times with students that week. Like my volunteers, I tried to connect with about five students regularly. I called each of them weekly and got together with each one of them about once a month.

Ricky was one of the students I connected with right away. His cousins had gone through my youth group, and his aunt asked me if I could keep an eye on him on his first day as a seventh grader. I introduced him to the other students and hung out with him during youth group time. After a few weeks I took him out for fries at one of the fast-food places in the area. As time progressed, I got to know Ricky fairly well. It was common to see Ricky at my house for dinner and in my car with me running errands all over town. I even got to be with Ricky the day he received Christ. That was a good day.

As time passed, Ricky moved to another school, and we saw less and less of each other. This concerned me because I knew he was starting to hang out with a rough group of friends. But he was in the hands of another youth worker, so I prayed God would take care of him. Eventually Ricky dropped off my radar. I felt guilty for letting that happen, and I often wondered what happened to Ricky.

Fast-forward 10 years.

I received an email about a month ago (as I sit here writing this). It was from someone who found me through my Web site:

> I'm emailing to see if I can get a hold of Jonathan McKee.
> I don't know if he remembers me. My name is Ricky, and
> I used to know him 10 years ago. He made a big impact
> in my life, and I'd like to talk with him. Thanks, Ricky

I wondered if this could be him. I wrote back to this "Ricky":

Is this the Ricky that's the cousin of Crystal and Melissa?
If it is… of course I remember you. Email me back or
call me.

I gave him my personal email and phone number. Sure enough, it was the same Ricky I'd spent so much time with, now happily married with two children and working with youth at his church.

Not long ago Ricky and I met for lunch, and he told me his story. Apparently those friends of his were bad news. Ricky explained how he made some bad decisions but knew God had something better.

Enter cute girl, stage left. God grabbed Ricky's attention with a girl. She was the daughter of a pastor and invited Ricky to church. To make a long story short, Ricky got back on track with God, and a few years later they got married.

Ricky told me, "I appreciate everything you did for me. You hung out with me, you had me over for dinner with your family, you took me to church—you even took me shopping for your wife's birthday." The now 25-year-old Ricky hugged me and thanked me for the time I'd invested in him. He couldn't remember a thing I'd said 10 years before, but he thanked me for spending time with him and loving him.

Loving students. Isn't that what youth ministry is about?

Les Christie, professor of youth ministry at William Jessup University, told me this simple truth: "The bottom line in youth ministry is to love students and love God."

USING TECHNOLOGY

Today's students are so immersed in technology that for many, face-to-screen relationships are replacing face-to-face relationships. But as we talked about in chapter one, this generation is becoming more isolated, having fewer close friendships than previous generations.

So how does technology come into play in regard to our interaction with students? Should we avoid it or use it? Should face-to-face contact replace or be partnered with technology?

In our efforts to connect with teenagers one-on-one, we will probably notice they are becoming less comfortable and less familiar with face-to-face communication. Ypulse.com's Anastasia Goodstein, a consultant, author, and expert on youth culture, recently commented about this phenomenon:

> I often get asked whether I think technology is replacing or diminishing real face-to-face intimacy. The truth is that being 'real' in person is very hard for a lot of teens.[vii]

Anastasia goes on to explain how teens often believe they're able to be "real" only through virtual alter egos. Many students don't know how to function in real life. Life for them is lived out vicariously as an avatar in an imaginary world where they can say what they want and be who they want to be.

I learned this firsthand in my research of the social networking Web site IMVU.com, a virtual hangout for teens and young adults. This Web site, advertising "Be Who You Want to Be," provides an arena of communication where authenticity is scarce. Every time I asked people their age, then told them mine, their answer would change.[viii]

It's ironic that a generation so adamant about "keeping it real" has lost the meaning of what authenticity is, often hiding behind a virtual cloak.

Researchers and doctors are now discovering it can be far more effective to use computers to collect data from teenagers because, initially, young people will type more on a screen than they will share face-to-face. In a recent study, doctors surveyed teenagers about subjects such as self-injury or feelings of depression. In face-to-face interviews, 52 percent of the students responded. That number went up to 69 percent when students could use a computer to respond.

> A teenager who is sad and maybe even considering suicide may be reluctant to tell a doctor about life-threatening troubles. But the same teenager is far more likely to tell a computer a secret he or she would be hesitant to share with even a close friend, much less a clinician who may be a friend of the family.[ix]

Digital Communication as a Stepping-Stone

We must not ignore the effectiveness of digital communication as a tool for relational ministry. But this doesn't mean we should shift *all* our relational efforts toward technology. The study we looked at in the first chapter reminds us technology does not typically help us grow deeper and more meaningful relationships. Remember…

- Students are more isolated.

- Students have fewer close friends.

- Students are drifting away from activities with personal interaction.

- Students are hurting more than ever before.

This increase in social isolation is creating a relational void in the lives of students today. We have an incredible opportunity to meet this need with something real, *face-to-face relationships*.

Even though teens might be more comfortable with us connecting with them through cell phones and computers, I see these digital mediums only as stepping-stones for youth workers to engage in face-to-face communication. This is not just because of the obvious value of face-to-face conversations, but also because of the increasing dangers emerging with technology. Legislation is changing regarding appropriate digital communication between adult mentors and students. (I'll touch on this in greater detail in chapter 13 when I talk about the boundaries and precautions we should consider with relational ministry.)

As we make connecting *one-on-one* a priority in our ministry, we may often utilize technology as a tool to transition toward more face-to-face conversations. In relational ministry, technology should be used as a tool, not a crutch.

3

THE ONE-ON-ONE INTENTIONS DEBATE

ALL ABOUT LOVE OR ALL ABOUT EVANGELISM?

Intentions has almost become a bad word.

"Are you really my friend...or do you have different _intentions_?"

It's important to consider our intentions when it comes to initiating contact with students. After all...are we seeking relationships with students because we truly care about them?

In my book _Getting Students to Show Up_, I make the following statement about our purpose in programming outreach events:

> The whole reason most of us do outreach events is so we
> can point people toward Jesus. I don't know about you, but
> I'm really not in the business of feeding teenagers pizza or

selling tickets to a basketball tournament. I want to impact students' lives with the life-changing message of Jesus Christ.[x]

Some people would say I've just revealed my "intentions." Like almost all discussions about ministry methodology, two polar-opposite points of view have surfaced:

THE "MR. KRABS" MINISTRY METHODOLOGY

These Christians are as adamant about sharing Christ as the popular cartoon character Mr. Krabs (from *SpongeBob SquarePants*) is about making money. Any Sponge Bob fan knows when Mr. Krabs is around, he's got an agenda: Everything he does is with the intention of getting richer.

Some Christians are that way about evangelism. The Mr. Krabs style of ministry proposes we should evangelize by *all means necessary*. People in favor of this methodology use numerous confrontational methods—tracts, surveys, and/or gimmicks—which supposedly help Christians introduce the subject of Jesus to others.

Years ago my son attended a Sunday school class where he was taught some of these methods. He was given a slick little tract that was a shiny cardstock image of a wallet with money sticking out of it. If someone placed this little item under a park bench or next to a picnic table, it would be easily mistaken for an actual wallet with money in it. Of course, once the unlikely prospect picked up this deceitful little tract and opened it, she was greeted with words that said something like, *"Don't be disappointed. Because what you have found is worth much more than any amount of money!"* Then the tract went on to share about God's love, sin, Jesus. You get the idea.

The Mr. Krabs method is focused on little else than end results. "We must share Jesus. Who cares who we turn away with our methods."

The obvious problem with this methodology is the fact that the casualties created usually far outweigh the positive results. Of course, people who support these methods will defend them by saying, "It's all worth it if even one person comes into the kingdom." Forget the fact that hundreds of people now *don't* want anything to do with Christians. But let's swing the pendulum to the opposite side of the continuum.

THE "NO STRINGS" MINISTRY METHODOLOGY

Another point of view has grown quite popular in the last decade, a method I call the "no strings" method. This is the opinion that "we just need to love others with no strings attached." People on this side of the coin will often cite biblical examples where Jesus healed or fed people—*with no altar call.* They are very critical of ministry models containing evangelistic intentions and often propose we should have no other intention but love itself.

My theory is that the "no strings" style has emerged as a reaction (or overreaction) to encounters with the Mr. Krabs evangelism mindset. It's not uncommon for people to feel driven to opposite extremes in order to find balance.

An influx of books has emerged that discusses the damage control needed after the Mr. Krabs method is used. Unfortunately, the pendulum has swung so far that sharing the gospel has almost become taboo. Evangelistic intentions are now frowned upon. After all, "shouldn't we just love others and let Jesus' love shine through us?"

Standing between the "Mr. Krabs" side and the "no strings" side, we're faced with what seems like one big, solitary choice: Do we follow the Great Commission—*Go and make disciples*—or the Great Commandment—*Love one another*?

Which point of view is right? Does our ministry have to be all about one or the other?

I believe the answer is a balance between both.

It's not either/or—it's both/and.

A BIBLICAL BALANCE

I must confess, after years of being surrounded by the Mr. Krabs methodology, I've definitely steered clear of any methods surrounding intense confrontation or trickery. But I've never swung so far as to stop sharing the gospel. I believe that in order to truly love students, I must share the life-saving truth about a God who loves them and wants a relationship with them.

In order to find answers on how to live out this balanced approach, I turned to the New Testament and read about Jesus and the early church.

Analyzing the Gospels, I started to dissect the example of Jesus himself. After all, both sides of this "intentions" debate are quoting him. The Mr. Krabs side quotes the Great Commission (Matthew 28:18-20) and verses like Luke 9:5: "If people do not welcome you, shake the dust off your feet when you leave their town, as a testimony against them."

The "no strings" viewpoint simply quotes the Great Commandment: *Love one another.* It argues that Christ loved people—and nothing else. (In other words, his points about narrow roads or "I am the way" don't matter as much.)

I've worked with churches that excelled at doing service projects: Feed the homeless. Rake leaves. Help the needy. These were all great projects. But then I noticed something: Some of these churches never—and I mean *never*—shared the gospel.

I asked people in some of these "no strings" churches why they just served the community and never shared the gospel. They usually replied, "Because that's what Jesus did."

Really?

It was these quotes from Jesus that prompted my thinking. I couldn't help but wonder, *What legacy did Jesus leave us?*

I examined Christ's actions and methods and documented every interaction the Bible recorded about the contact Christ had with others (this was no small task). I tried to keep my eyes on the big picture of the Gospels while continuing to pay attention to Jesus' own relational approach. I created a table and took notes as I read the four Gospels. I cited the Scripture (column 1), noted the context (column 2), and marked the audience (column 3). My goal was to get a good glimpse of what was going on when I looked back at my notes in the table. Sometimes these interactions were as small as a paragraph, and others were pages long. But, to the best of my ability, I tried to count each interaction with an individual or group as one occurrence. For example, the Sermon on the Mount (although it may have been a collection of sermons) counted as one interaction. Conversely, when Jesus walked through a town, he often had encounters with multiple people. I counted each of those conversations or interactions as individual occurrences.

Then I created columns noting what action was taken, if any (column 4), and if a message or central idea was communicated (column 5). To sum up my findings about each encounter, I included a final column (column 6) that answered the question, "Did Jesus bring up 'God stuff' or not?"

My desire in this study was to discover a more accurate picture of Jesus' encounters with people. Here's a glimpse of what this study looked like: (An extended sample of my study is the appendix).

Jesus' Encounters

Scripture	Context	Audience	Action Taken	Message Communicated (if any)	Did he bring up "God stuff"
Matt. 3:13-17	Jesus is baptized	People of Jerusalem, Judea, & the Jordan region	Jesus allows John the Baptist to baptize him	Jesus replied, "Let it be so now; it is proper for us to do this to fulfill all righteousness." Then John consented. (v.15, NIV)	Yes, I consider referring to "the fulfillment of all righteousness" God stuff.
Matt. 4:1-11	Jesus is tempted by Satan	Satan	Jesus used Scripture to defend against temptation	I'm so much more than flesh and blood—I'm a spiritual being. No way.	Yes, he quoted Scripture, rebuking Satan.
Matt. 4:12-17	Jesus goes to Galilee, then Capernaum.	All the people "from that time on" (v.17).	Preaching	From that time on Jesus began to preach, "Repent, for the kingdom of heaven is near." (v.17, NIV)	Yes, he brought a message from God that said, "Turn from your own ways and turn to God."

You may also want to do a simplified version of this study yourself. Find two highlighters (green and red will work). Read through the Gospels and mark a green dot wherever Jesus brings up God or the truth of the Scriptures. Mark a red dot if he simply loves people with acts of compassion or service.

My wife Lori and I both did this study across the Gospels. As I finished studying, it was clear that Jesus was not afraid to share truth (a lot of green dots). Sometimes he met people's physical needs (red dots), sometimes he preached, and sometimes he did both. Some people were ready to hear the truth, and others sought him out with questions they had.

I believe some of us forget this balance that Christ modeled. The more the "Mr. Krabs" people read the Gospels with open eyes, the more they see how much Jesus cared for people as a whole. The more the "no strings" people read the Gospels with hearing ears, the more they will notice how often Jesus wasn't afraid to preach the hard truth.

People might sway to one side or the other—that's to be expected. Some people have the gift of hospitality while others have the gift of prophecy. But that doesn't mean preachers shouldn't be hospitable or those who love serving others should use their gifts as an excuse to keep quiet.

The answer to the intentions debate is to maintain a balance of both love and truth.

After studying Jesus' ministry, I decided to study the early church and Paul. In Acts chapter six we see an interesting situation develop which provides a great example of this balancing act.

> In those days when the number of disciples was increasing, the Hellenistic Jews among them complained against the Hebraic Jews because their widows were being overlooked in the daily distribution of food. So the Twelve gathered all the disciples together and said, "It would not be right for us to neglect the ministry of the word of God in order to wait on tables. Brothers and sisters, choose seven men from among you who are known to be full of the Spirit and wisdom. We will turn this responsibility over to them and will give our attention to prayer and the ministry of the word. (Acts 6:1-4)

The early church was engaged in a vital social program helping local widows. But apparently this program needed a little more attention and management. So the "New 12" (complete with Matthias, Judas' replacement) got together to choose some wise leaders to help manage the program.

Think about this for a moment: The early church was showing love by caring for the community, particularly widows. (The "no strings" group probably loves this—a perfect example of the church reaching out in action.) Meanwhile, the disciples were focused on "the ministry of the word of God." But they needed someone to help with this "love-in-action" program. It might be that they perceived these two foci as requiring different gifts.

Look who the disciples chose to run the "love-in-action" program.

> This proposal pleased the whole group. They chose Stephen, a man full of faith and of the Holy Spirit; also Philip, Procorus, Nicanor, Timon, Parmenas, and Nicolas from Antioch, a convert to Judaism. They presented them to the apostles, who prayed and laid their hands on them.
> (Acts 6:5-6)

Check out the list of guys they chose. Sure, if you were reading the book of Acts from start to finish for the first time, those names wouldn't jump out at you. But anyone who has read Acts even once probably recognizes the first two names on this list of "social workers" assigned to distribute food: Stephen and Philip.

Let me ask you a question: When you think of Stephen and Philip, what do you picture? Food servers?

I don't know about you, but when I think of Stephen, I see a man of God who preached one of the boldest messages about Christ in history—a message that cost him his life (Acts 6:8–7:60). Stephen was obviously someone who cared for people. But he also balanced that with conversations about Christ—bold conversations. When people of different beliefs began to argue with Stephen, Acts 6:10 says "they could not stand up against his wisdom or the Spirit by whom he spoke."

What about Philip? When I think of Philip, I see a man who went to Samaria and proclaimed Christ (Acts 8:10). I see a man who preached to a region that had always followed Simon the Sorcerer.

> But when they believed Philip as he proclaimed the good news of the kingdom of God and the name of Jesus Christ, they were baptized, both men and women. Simon himself believed and was baptized. And he followed Philip everywhere, astonished by the great signs and miracles he saw. (Acts 8:12-13)

When I think of Philip, I see a man so motivated by the Holy Spirit that he ran alongside the chariot of an important Ethiopian leader to initiate a conversation with him about Christ. Philip led the Ethiopian official to Christ and baptized him right alongside the road.

Do these guys sound like they are just "loving others," never bringing up the gospel?

We aren't supposed to make a choice between the Great Commission (*go and make disciples*) and the Great Commandment (*love one another*). It's not either/or; it's both/and. The answer to the intentions debate is to maintain a balance of both.

As we build relationships with students, we need to love them for who they are, whether they choose to live for Jesus or not. But part of loving them is sharing God's truth with them. That means being prepared for those opportunities (1 Peter 3:15-18) and listening to the Holy Spirit's prompting.

Don't be like Mr. Krabs, trying to achieve another notch in your evangelism belt while remaining blind to people's needs. And don't overreact and assume that loving "no strings attached" means never talking about God.

ALL ABOUT LOVE AND ALL ABOUT EVANGELISM

My brother Thom and his wife Amy used to volunteer for Youth for Christ in Sacramento, where they ran a weekly Campus Life Club in their house. Often with Campus Life Clubs, the first group of students you contact steers the direction of what type of students the group will attract. In my brother's case, he had a heart to minister to students who were outcasts and marginalized at the school.

It was there Thom met Enrique, a student searching for answers to big questions. Thom and Amy are not only gifted in compassion and hospitality, but they are intellectuals. They often found themselves in deep conversations with students about issues such as politics, world religions, and the meaning of life. Enrique would talk with Thom until the late hours about his beliefs, passions, and struggles. He shared about how he'd been experimenting with same-sex encounters.

As Thom built a relationship with Enrique, he often used these discussions to share about his relationship with Christ. Enrique was interested in Jesus but hesitant to put his trust in him because of the reputations of Christians.

Enrique had an uncle who was "out" regarding his gay lifestyle, living with his partner in San Francisco. His uncle never had good experiences with Christians. Enrique was very close to him and valued his opinion. Unfortunately, that opinion was always, "Stay away from Christians. They are a hateful, intolerant group."

In the middle of the school year, Thom and Amy had a party for all their Campus Life students and their families. This uncle showed up at the party with his partner. Thom struggled internally when he saw him because he was so frustrated with what this guy had become in Enrique's life. But he suppressed his frustration and welcomed them into his house.

Thom spent most of the evening with the uncle and his partner, talking and playing pool. Thom had lived in San Francisco for a year in college, so they discussed the city and all the best restaurants. He actually found it quite easy to talk with them. The evening passed, and everyone had a great time.

A few months later Enrique went on a Campus Life trip and heard the gospel presented again. Enrique approached Thom and said, "Okay, I know the lifestyle I've been experimenting with is wrong. I need forgiveness. I need Jesus." Tom talked through the gospel with Enrique one-on-one, making sure that he understood each point: *God's love, our sin, Jesus paying for our sin, and what it truly means to put our trust in him, giving Jesus license to transform us.* Enrique listened carefully, processing all of what Thom shared. Finally, Thom asked him again, "Are you ready to put your trust in Jesus?" Enrique nodded that he was ready and prayed, asking for forgiveness of his sins and putting his faith in Christ.

As Thom discipled Enrique, he encouraged him, "I think it would be good for you to tell your friends about this commitment you made. What do you think?" Thom and Enrique spent quite a while talking about who he might tell and what that might look like. It was then Thom mentioned, "How about telling your uncle?" Thom was sure this encounter would be difficult, especially because Enrique had made a decision not to engage in homosexual activity.

A week later Thom and Enrique met again. Thom was eager to hear about Enrique's experiences. "How did it go?" Enrique began sharing with Thom about every encounter with his friends. Thom listened patiently, but eventually cut to the chase. "How did it go with your uncle?" Thom was leaning forward in his chair in anticipation.

"Oh, it went great," Enrique said matter-of-factly.

Thom was shocked. "It went great? You mean—he was okay with it?"

"Yeah," Enrique responded. "He was happy for me."

Thom was thoroughly confused. His face must have revealed as much, because Enrique began to explain.

"A few months ago my uncle's partner was hospitalized. He has been HIV positive for years, but now he has been diagnosed with full-blown AIDS.

My uncle has been visiting his partner every night at the hospital. He's the only visitor. All of his partner's family have abandoned him; my uncle seems to be his only true friend. So each night he'd go and sit by the bedside.

Apparently, one night when my uncle showed up there was a nice old lady sitting by the bedside wiping his partner's face with a cool washcloth. He had no idea who this lady was. She wasn't wearing a nurse's outfit, so he asked her. She said she was part of a local church group volunteering at the hospital each week taking care of AIDS patients. She asked if he minded—my uncle was astonished.

This lady began visiting my uncle's partner regularly, caring for him and talking with him about Jesus. Eventually his partner became a Christian."

Enrique smiled. "When I told my uncle I became a Christian, he told me, 'Good. Because those people have an amazing capacity to love like no other.'"

I never heard what eventually happened with Enrique's uncle. But Thom walked away from that experience even more convinced about the power of the love of Christ reflected in the life of his true followers. That kind of love, balanced with a willingness to share about the source of that love, can truly change lives.

4
CONNECTING WITH SIX TYPES OF STUDENTS ONE-ON-ONE

I've found it helpful to divide what we do in ministry into two categories: *outreach* and *discipleship*.

Outreach is connecting with people who don't know Jesus and pointing them to him through words and actions. *Discipleship* is helping believers grow closer to Jesus and live more like him.

Most of the students we encounter fall into one of these two categories: *Outreach students* (the ones who don't know Jesus) and *discipleship students* (the ones who, at some time or another, made a decision to follow Jesus).

As such, our one-on-one time will differ with students from each of these two categories. Our focus with *outreach students* will be more evangelistic. They need Christ. Our *discipleship students*, however, need to understand how to live out their faith day to day.

Some of you are already wondering if I am oversimplifying. Are we to assume all *outreach students* are the same? Similarly, do all *discipleship students* have the same attitudes and needs? Don't some students show greater spiritual maturity than others? With that in mind, these categories actually appear pretty broad, don't they?

Perhaps we should look a little deeper at each of these two categories.

DIVERSE ATTITUDES

Her name was Sierra. I first met her at lunch when I was visiting her campus. She didn't hesitate to ask me, "What are you doing here?" She wanted to know why some stranger was visiting her school.

Before I could even answer, she blurted out another question. "Are you gonna invite me to some church thing? Because if you are, don't bother. I'm an atheist, and I'll never go."

I was at a loss for words, probably because I was still trying to figure out how she knew I was from a church. One thing was very clear: This girl had issues with God and church.

I didn't meet a lot of Sierras on campus. The most typical student was like James. I met him at a football game. When he found out I was a youth pastor, he just smiled and said, "Oh—I don't *do* church."

I also responded with a smile, "Well, you're not alone. But what's your reason?"

He laughed, responding, "I'm always in bed on Sunday mornings." Then he was quick to clarify, "But I'm cool with God and all that."

James' response is typical of many from this generation. *I'm cool with God; I just don't need church.*

As emblematic as James is, not every non-church attender is against the idea of church. Chris, for example, came to church with me the first time I invited him. He was quick to tell me, "Yeah, I've been meaning to go to church. I'm kind of interested in spiritual stuff right now."

I met all three of these students outside the church walls. Sierra, James, and Chris had never attended a church more than once or twice in their entire lives. None of them knew Jesus, so it's probably safe to assume they were all *outreach students.*

Each of these *outreach students* had different attitudes about God and the church. It's hard to make broad generalizations about all students who don't know God or attend church because the differences are much too great.

Similarly, it would be crazy to assume all *discipleship students* are alike regarding their responses to God and the church. We've all met students who've accepted Christ but don't seem to take faith seriously. Meanwhile, other students are eager to grow and learn how to live out their faith day to day.

These differences remind me of Jesus' parable of the sower in Matthew 13:3-8. This is the parable about the farmer who went out to sow his seed.

> Then he told them many things in parables, saying: "A farmer went out to sow his seed. As he was scattering the seed, some fell along the path, and the birds came and ate it up. Some fell on rocky places, where it did not have much soil. It sprang up quickly, because the soil was shallow. But when the sun came up, the plants were scorched, and they withered because they had no root. Other seed fell among thorns, which grew up and choked the plants. Still other seed fell on good soil, where it produced a crop—a hundred, sixty or thirty times what was sown.

Those of us who have been working with students for a few years have probably heard many different reactions to the gospel message. Some reject the gospel all together. Some might seem to accept it at first, but it never really seems to take root. Others grow quickly and produce incredible fruit.

So how can we effectively minister to such diverse types of students? How do we meet all these needs?

One thing is clear: There's no "one size fits all" way to reach out to students, introduce them to Christ, and help them grow in faith. So where do we begin?

SIX TYPES OF STUDENTS

In my ministry experience I've encountered six types of students: Three kinds of *outreach students* and three kinds of *discipleship students.*

SIX TYPES OF STUDENTS

Outreach			Discipleship		
No Way	Not Interested	Checking Things Out	Stagnant	Growing	Looking for Ministry

Hopefully your ministry puts you in a position where you encounter all six types of these students. Let's look briefly at each type:

The *No-Way Kid*

The first student is the one I call the *no-way kid*, simply because this student is quick to tell you there is "no way" you'll ever see him at church.

Sierra, the girl I previously described, is a perfect example of a *no-way kid*. "Are you gonna invite me to some church thing? Because if you are, don't bother. I'm an atheist, and I'll never go."

Surprisingly, there are a lot fewer atheists than you might think. According to the U.S. Religious Landscape Survey from Pew Forum on Religion and Public Life, 25% of young adults (ages 18 to 29) claim to be unaffiliated with a religion. This percentage is definitely larger than before, but within this number, only 3% are atheist, 4% are agnostic, and 18% simply say they are generally "unaffiliated" when it comes to religion or spirituality. There's a small number of young people who truly believe "there is no God!"[xi]

No-way kids aren't always atheists; they might believe in God and even consider themselves close to him. But if they are like most of America, they don't feel they need church.

No-way kids are not impossible to reach. I've seen numerous *no-way kids* give their lives to Christ. How? Usually because someone invested in them *one-on-one*.

The next chapter is devoted entirely to the *no-way kid*. We'll discuss a little more about the *no-way* mindset and how and where we can connect with these students.

The *Not-Interested Kid*

The *not-interested kid* is probably the most common student *not* at church on Sunday. It's not because he has anything against God or the Bible—he'd just rather be *anywhere else*.

Sometimes we have these students in our youth groups or Sunday school classes. Does this surprise you? Just think about it for a moment. *Not-interested kids* are sometimes forced to go to church by their parents or grandparents. They are present, but they wish they were somewhere else.

Some of us have never considered that we might have a *not-interested kid* (or a *no-way kid*, for that matter) in our youth groups. I don't know about you, but these types of students make me think twice about my talks and curriculum.

Most *not-interested kids* are like James, "Oh, I don't *do* church. I'm always in bed on Sunday mornings. But I'm cool with God and all that."

In other words: *I'm cool with God; I just don't need church.* *Not-interested kids* are not without hope. Usually a relationship can help change their preconceived ideas about Jesus, the church, and Christians. That's what eventually happened with James. After hanging out with me for about three months, James finally gave in and came to church with me. He didn't love getting up on Sunday morning, but he actually enjoyed the music and liked the people he met. I could see it on his face. It was nothing like he expected.

One thing I realized after spending considerable time with *not-interested kids*...they don't usually want to come to our stuff. (Hence the "Not-Interested" moniker.) Unfortunately that's the number-one evangelism tool many of us rely on: *Inviting kids to our stuff.* Perhaps some of us need to break free from this crutch and learn how to connect with *not-interested kids* on *their* turf.

I've devoted chapter six to connecting with the *Not-interested kid.*

The *Checking-Things-Out Kid*

Earlier I mentioned there were three kinds of *outreach students—* students who don't know Christ yet. You've met two types so far. I call the third type of student the *checking-things-out kid.* This student is willing to give church a try and shows an interest in spiritual conversations. He isn't resistant to "checking things out."

Chris is a perfect example of a *checking-things-out kid.* Chris was introduced to me after school by one of my student leaders.

"This is my youth pastor."

Amazingly, Chris didn't flinch (believe me, some do). We talked for a while in front of the school and he quickly turned the conversation to my job. He seemed curious about church. The door was open (and it was after school hours—I'd given my word to the administration never to bring up God or church during school hours), so I invited him. He was quick to tell me, "Yeah, I've been meaning to go to church. I'm kind of interested in spiritual stuff right now."

I'm amazed how many students will come to church if simply invited.

Years ago I read a statistic that reported an enormous percentage of people would come to church if just asked. I set out to see if that was true about my community. In my experiment fewer than 50 percent of my invitees agreed to try attending church.

Over the years I've discovered a way to help more people become open to coming to church: *One-on-one attention.* The more time we invested in students relationally, the more likely they would come to church and engage in spiritual conversations.

This isn't that surprising if you think about it. Who do you think is more likely to go to church with you or open up about deep issues—a friend or a stranger?

One-on-one conversations break down relational walls. Relational ministry opens doors to deeper conversations.

Do you have any contact with *outreach students?* I think we all should. Look at Jesus' ministry. He spent a huge amount of time with crowds of unbelievers, even dining with "notorious sinners."

But what about the students who have already accepted Christ? I call these *discipleship students,* and I see three types.

The *Stagnant Kid*

The *stagnant kid* is one who made a decision to follow Christ at some point but never really grew in faith. He's the seed that was trampled or grew for a short time but was choked by weeds or withered away.

The *stagnant kid* usually struggles with getting plugged into church. He might slip in and out of youth group without being noticed. He has failed to commit to a Bible study or small group, so he isn't connected with other students or growing in faith.

However, *stagnant kids* usually will come out for fun events. If it's fun, they come. If it's deep, they'll vanish.

One-on-one attention does wonders for the *stagnant kid.* What many of these students need is someone who'll disciple them, helping them understand a deeper faith.

Some of Jesus' final words on earth give us a picture of what our main ministry goal should be.

> Therefore go and **make disciples** of all nations, baptizing them in the name of the Father and of the Son and of the Holy Spirit, and teaching them to obey everything I have commanded you. And surely I am with you always, to the very end of the age. (Matthew 28:19-20, NIV, emphasis mine)

Jesus asked us to go and make disciples. Discipleship is a lot of work, and some of the most effective discipleship happens *one-on-one.*

In my ministries I've always tried to be proactive about discipleship. When students placed their trust in Christ, we immediately gave them Bibles and made appointments to start discipling them. At that first appointment (usually at a fast-food joint), we'd set up a weekly time to meet and decide what we would be reading. Sometimes I took new believers through one of the Gospels (usually Mark). Other times I used a discipleship workbook like *Welcome to the Family,* the free one on our ministry's Web site.

Our goals for a *stagnant kid* were always to disciple and transform him or her into a *growing kid,* plugged into church and growing in faith.

We'll spend chapter nine on *stagnant kids*, outlining some ways to initiate contact with them, disciple them, and help plug them in to church.

The *Growing Kid*

Growing kids are exactly who we want our *stagnant kids* to become: connected to God's people (the church) and growing in their relationships with Jesus.

Growing kids aren't perfect. They still might talk during your message, cuss when they stub their toes, and even have a couple of explicit songs on their iPods. But they've put their trust in Jesus, and they are slowly allowing him to transform their minds. Like all believers, they are a work in progress.

Growing kids usually go to a Bible study and/or attend a small group. Their faith is important to them, and they are open (sometimes even eager) to learn how they can grow each day.

These students need to begin to discover their spiritual gifts. Once believers discover their spiritual gifts and are given opportunities to serve, look out! They are on their way to becoming the sixth type of student, the *looking-for-ministry kid*.

We'll be spending an entire chapter on the *growing kid* as well, providing insight to connecting with them and helping them discover their spiritual gifts for service.

The *Looking-for-Ministry Kid*

The *looking-for-ministry kids* are your student leaders. Don't let the word *leader* confuse you. That doesn't mean they are always up front or naturally gregarious (i.e., the life of the party). Leaders can have the gifts of hospitality or compassion. They might serve behind the scenes. Regardless, they are mature in their faith and are looking for opportunities to minister in everyday situations.

You will be amazed at the impact your *looking-for-ministry kids* can make if you equip them to love *outreach students*, connect with them, and engage in spiritual conversations. Some of your *looking-for-ministry kids* are already friends with *outreach students*. They play soccer, attend classes, and live on the same streets as *outreach students*. They don't have the barriers we have. For them, steps toward connection have already been made.

Looking-for-ministry kids are the ones who will become your next youth ministry volunteers when they graduate. Some ministries will use older high school students from this group to minister to junior high students or be camp counselors.

We will devote chapter *eleven* to these students, looking at how *one-on-one* time can help this group become stronger in faith and encouraged in areas of giftedness.

THE SIX TYPES OF STUDENTS IN YOUR MINISTRY

As you meet students in your community and church, you'll probably find they fit into one of these six categories. You might have already been mentally placing names of students into these categories. *Let's see, where would Michael and Taylor be? And what about Tim, Chris, Natalie, and Ashley?*

If you were to place your students in this table, it might look something like this:

SIX TYPES OF STUDENTS

Outreach			Discipleship		
No Way	Not Interested	Checking Things Out	Stagnant	Growing	Looking for Ministry
Michael			Natalie		
	Taylor			Tim	
		Chris			Ashley

Have you met all six types of students? Most likely your students aren't this neatly spread out. Some might even be beween categories. For the sake of simplicity, let's use this as an example:

SIX TYPES OF STUDENTS

Outreach			Discipleship		
No Way	Not Interested	Checking Things Out	Stagnant	Growing	Looking for Ministry
		Morgan T.J.	David Alyssa Brandon	Tyler Dillon Rebecca	

Some of us might not know students from each one of these categories. If you honestly can't name a single *no-way kid*, then you might want to ask yourself why. Do you visit your local campus? Do you ever attend community sports events? Do you coach or tutor? Do you have any outreach activities or events that draw any of the three types of *outreach students*? Are some of these types of students forced to go to your church by their parents? Where could you go to encounter more *outreach students*?

Similarly, if you can only think of one or two *looking-for-ministry kids*, ask yourself why. Why aren't your students developing into leaders? Do you have a student-leadership program? Do you provide opportunities to serve? Do you train students how to reach out to their friends?

If we find our ministries are missing some of these students, we might need to reevaluate the reach of our ministries (we'll talk more about this in the final chapter—Instilling the Value of *One-on-One* in Your Ministry).

If your ministry makes *one-on-one* time a priority with all six types of these students, you will start to see incredible fruit. If you and your volunteers are spending face-to-face time with all six of these types of students, you will begin to see students putting their trust in Jesus and growing in faith. When this happens, your table will change. You will see names start to move to the right.

This brings up a very important principle when using this table as a tool to assess your ministry: *Your goal should be moving students toward growth and ministry.*

MOVING STUDENTS TOWARD DISCIPLESHIP

As you can see, the use of this tool will help you observe and track the process of salvation and spiritual growth. As students become more interested in becoming like Christ, you'll notice them moving to the right—toward discipleship, growth, and ministry.

As students become Christians and move from being *outreach students* to *discipleship students*, our hope is they will skip the *stagnant* stage and move right to growth. Unfortunately, some students do become *stagnant*. Most youth ministry veterans have had the experience of leading a student to Christ, only to see her fail to get plugged into discipleship or a Bible study. We'll talk about ways to help prevent this in chapter nine: *The stagnant kid.*

When an *outreach student* becomes a *discipleship student*, our desire is always to start discipling this new believer immediately and help facilitate connection with other Christians. When this happens, the *discipleship student* becomes a *growing kid.*

Maybe one of your volunteers, Heidi, noticed Natalie was a *stagnant kid* and began spending time with her. Heidi took her shopping and for ice cream a few times. Then she took her to dinner once on youth group night and offered to take her to youth group afterward. This was key because Natalie hadn't been attending youth group. At youth group Heidi hung out with Natalie and introduced her to other girls. She made sure Natalie was placed in her small group. Before long Natalie became plugged in to the group and showed interest in growing in her faith.

Natalie can now be moved to the right—she's now a *growing kid*.

SIX TYPES OF STUDENTS

Outreach			Discipleship		
No Way	Not Interested	Checking Things Out	Stagnant	Growing	Looking for Ministry
Michael	Taylor	Chris	Natalie ⟶	→ Natalie Tim	Ashley

The purpose of this table is quite clear. Assess your students and try to move them to the right. We want to see *outreach students* put their trust in Jesus and become *discipleship students*. We want to see *not-interested kids* become *checking-things-out kids*. We want to see *stagnant kids* become *growing kids* and *growing kids* become *looking-for-ministry kids*. We'll see how this process happens with each student in the next six chapters.

It doesn't happen overnight. As you know, evangelism and discipleship take time. It might take years for some people. But the fact is, much of it is accomplished *one-on-one*.

UNCOVERING THE TRUTH

Take a few minutes and place your students on this table. (You can make a copy of the blank version of this chart in the appendix of this book. We will also provide more time to explore this chart with your volunteer leaders in the last chapter.)

Outreach			Discipleship		
No Way	Not Interested	Checking Things Out	Stagnant	Growing	Looking for Ministry

Using this chart to assess your group will accomplish several things:

It might help you realize you don't know your students as much as you thought you did.

You might not know which column they belong in. So how do you find out? You obviously don't walk up to them and say, "Hey, which column are you in?" If we don't know where students belong in this table, we need to get to know them better. And guess how you do that?

Yep, you guessed it. *One-on-one.*

IMPORTANT NOTE: This tool isn't meant to show students where they are spiritually. This table is for your eyes only (and the eyes of your adult leaders). Students most likely will be upset by the notion that their spirituality is being tracked on a chart. So emphasize to your leaders to be careful to keep this private. It could be damaging if a student accidently sees a chart that is left out.

Placing students in this table helps you realize the needs they have.

Assessing the needs of your students gives you and your volunteers attainable goals. *Outreach students* need Christ, and we need to know how to share Christ with students *one-on-one*.

Stagnant kids need to be discipled and plugged in. *Growing kids* not only need to be discipled, but they also need to discover their spiritual gifts so they can begin to minister to others.

This table will not only help us realize the needs our students have...

This table will help build accountability and motivate you toward further investment in your group.

As you minister to the students in your group, you *should* see students moving to the right on the table.

I'm amazed how many youth workers will use sheer numbers to evaluate how effective their ministry is. "We had sixty last night."

Sixty what? Sixty students who came out for free pizza? The important question is, what are you doing with those sixty students?

That's where this table really helps. I love doing free pizza events and bringing out sixty students. The question is, *what are you going to do now that you've made first contact with them?*

This table holds us accountable for facilitating life-changing ministry.

There's nothing magical about this table. This is simply a tool I've used to help me analyze the scope of my ministry and accurately assess how I'm meeting the spiritual needs of the students in my ministry area. I've taught similar methods across the country, and hundreds of ministries have found it helpful. I think you might find it will help you as well.

In the final chapter I explain step-by-step how your entire ministry team can use this tool to remain accountable in your goal to connect with and reach out to students.

SIMILAR *AND* DIFFERENT

I've encountered all six types of students and sat *one-on-one* with each of them. It's amazing how similar *and* different these students are. No, that wasn't a typo: Similar and different. Surface conversations with students start very similarly. It's not surprising. Many of these students are spending enormous amounts of time in front of the same media sources, almost enough time weekly for a full-time job. That's why when I travel to cities all over North America, students look and sound alike.

But when I sit down with students *one-on-one*, differences in these six types of students emerge. Heredity and environment come into play, world views come out, and the scars of life experience show their toll.

Often we'll never discover these things if we don't allow time for *one-on-one* connection.

CONNECTING WITH OUTREACH STUDENTS

Outreach			Discipleship		
No Way	Not Interested	Checking Things Out	Stagnant	Growing	Looking for Ministry

The next three chapters are devoted to connecting with *outreach students.*

Each of the three types of *outreach students* has unique characteristics, but the process of connecting with each student is very similar. As we embark into these chapters, we're going to examine the similarities and differences between each type of student. I'm going to build each chapter on the previous one, cumulatively.

The *no-way kid* is the hardest student to make first contact with. So we'll cover "first contact" thoroughly and exclusively in chapter five. Then we'll continue exploring the process of building relationships with another type of *outreach student*, the *not-interested kid,* in chapter six. Finally, in chapter seven we will focus on the *checking-things-out kids,* with the hopes of helping these students find life in Christ and move toward discipleship.

5
ONE-ON-ONE
WITH THE
NO-WAY KID

Outreach			Discipleship		
No Way	Not Interested	Checking Things Out	Stagnant	Growing	Looking for Ministry

DESCRIPTION:

The *no-way kid* is resistant to church, Christians, and sometimes God. He is usually vocal about his feelings against Christianity, sometimes to the point of belligerence. I call him the *no-way kid* simply because this student is quick to tell you there is "no way" you'll ever see him at church.

OUR GOALS WITH THE *NO-WAY KID*:

Our hope with a *no-way kid* is to befriend him, listen to him, and try to figure out why he is so bitter against church or Christianity in general. Once we build a relationship, we hope he's willing to *check things out* (engage in spiritual conversations, visit a venue where those conversations happen, or visit a place where he can hear spiritual truths).

"How would you describe yourself?"

That's the question Rick asked her. She seemed to be the center of attention at this particular picnic table by the softball field. She raised her eyes to meet his gaze without moving her head. "If Satan was a female—that's me!"

Her retort was packed with meaning, subtle and obvious. Her rebellious outer shell was just a cover for a damaged self-esteem. She craved for people to notice her and had learned to settle for negative attention. After all, it was much easier to harness.

Rick didn't hesitate. He had encountered numerous students just like her in his years running an on-campus ministry at this particular high school. "That's great," he replied with a smile. "You're exactly the kind of person I like meeting."

No-way kids aren't always so verbal about their objections to God or the church. But they usually have their minds made up. "There's no way you'll ever get me to your church thing."

No-way kids are probably the most difficult to connect with of all six types of students. They are usually not on your turf—you have to go find them. Furthermore, they are probably suspicious of your intentions. If you want to share Christ's love with students, then they don't want any part of it.

Don't be discouraged—I have some really good news. Once you build a relationship with a *no-way kid*, that usually changes.

My friend Rob directs a Campus Life ministry out of a barn down the street from a local high school. Rob visits campus regularly and effectively connects with all kinds of *outreach students*, including a growing number of *no-way kids*. Recently he told me something fascinating. "I've never had a student who I built a relationship with say *no* to church."

Think about that for a second. *Never had a student say no*. Rob is 100 percent successful at bringing students to church once he has earned their trust. Once Rob connects with students, they are willing to give church a try. Relationships open doors.

The error many evangelists make with *no-way kids* is trying to convert them through arguing. I've seen it hundreds of times. "Just read this book on apologetics and argue them into the kingdom right there on the spot!" That method doesn't work on this generation of young people, especially the *no-way kid* (my friend Dan Kimball expands on this in great detail in his book, *They Like Jesus, But Not the Church*, Zondervan, 2007[xii]).

Relationships, however, break down these walls. Ministries with workers who care about students as a whole and invest in them relationally notice these students gradually become open to spiritual conversations, and many of them eventually give their lives to Christ.

I had a *no-way kid* in my ministry named Carly. She let me know first thing she was an atheist and wanted nothing to do with church. She was surprised when she saw her beliefs didn't bother me a bit.

For a year my volunteers and I invested in Carly. She came to our fun campus activities and even a few retreats where we talked about God. As she became closer to us, she became more open to these conversations.

Eventually, she came to a large outreach event where she heard the gospel. I'll never forget watching her go forward and give her life to Christ. Later, I asked her what finally changed her mind. She said, "I've been hearing you guys talk about it for a year now, and I've been trying to tell myself it's not true. But I'm just tired of not believing."

A relational investment can yield spiritual results. *No-way kids* don't need to be argued with—they need to be loved.

So it seems the big question is: How do we begin relationships with *no-way kids*?

DISCOVERING CULTURE, ATTITUDES, AND TRENDS

Reaching out to any particular group of people should always begin with a commitment to understanding culture. Missionaries to China, Romania, or Kenya spend months studying the culture and language before embarking on their missions experiences. Yet youth workers, both volunteer and paid, seem to think they don't need to know much about American teenage culture, apparently because it's their own culture. They must have concluded that things haven't changed much in the last 5, 10, or 20 years. But culture in America is always changing.

Becoming educated about today's teens is a continual process. Youth workers should be proactive in learning about youth culture. Maybe that's as simple as reading youth ministry newsletters like the weekly YS Update from www.YouthSpecialties.com or the weekly Youth Culture Window articles our ministry provides at www.TheSource4YM.com. Some of us might even like more in-depth resources like I provide in my blog on the same Web site, or like those from Generation Y expert Anastasia Goodstein at www.YPulse.com. My friend Walt Mueller also has an entire Web site devoted to understanding today's youth culture at www.CPYU.org.

As I write this book, I can honestly say the *no-way kid*'s attitude hasn't changed all that much in the last few decades. Don't get me wrong; technology has changed greatly, shifting the way students spend time and express opinions. The number of unchurched people has increased as well. More and more are exiting the church.[xiii] In 1991 there were 39 million unchurched Americans compared with 75 million in 2004. But despite all these changes, *no-way kids* seem to have similar frustrations with God and church as they did almost 20 years ago. In 1993 Lee Strobel admitted that as an atheist, he was morally adrift but secretly wanted an anchor.[xiv] In a personal interview with him, he told me he always knew God was real. He just suppressed that truth, knowing that admitting God's reality would require a change in lifestyle.

I believe there are no true atheists, only proclaimed atheists. I believe Paul's letter to the Romans supports this idea:

> The wrath of God is being revealed from heaven against all the godlessness and wickedness of human beings who suppress the truth by their wickedness, since what may be known about God is plain to them, because God has made it plain to them. For since the creation of the world God's invisible qualities—his eternal power and divine nature—have been clearly seen, being understood from what has been made, so that people are without excuse. (Romans 1:18-20)

Whenever I meet a *no-way kid*, I am comforted by the fact that deep down they likely do know God is real, regardless of what they assert publicly.

But as we note in chapter four, atheists and agnostics only comprise 7 percent of young adults. *No-way kids* aren't always atheists; they might believe in God and even consider themselves close to him. But if they are like most of America, they don't feel the need to be a part of a church, and they don't think the Bible has all the answers.

USA Today recently released a summary of the 2008 Pew Forum on Religion & Public Life's U.S. Religious Landscape Survey.[xv] The survey of 35,000 people revealed some interesting findings about U.S. religious beliefs. A few highlights:

- 92 percent of U.S. adults believe in God

- 78 percent overall say there are "absolute standards of right and wrong"

- 74 percent say "there is a heaven, where people who have led good lives are eternally rewarded"

- 58 percent say they pray at least once a day

Those findings are pretty positive. But dig a little deeper.

- Only 29 percent of the same group rely on their religion to delineate these "absolute standards of right and wrong." The majority (52 percent) turn to "practical experience and common sense," with 9 percent relying on philosophy and reason, and 5 percent on scientific information.

- 70 percent say "many religions can lead to eternal life"

- Only 59 percent say there's a "hell, where people who have led bad lives and die without being sorry are eternally punished"

The *USA Today* article went on to conclude, "Religion today in the USA is a salad bar where people heap on upbeat beliefs they like and often leave the veggies—like strict doctrines—behind."

I've noticed some of the same trends over the last decade. God is okay. Faith is okay. Heaven is okay. But don't tell me Jesus is the only way, don't tell me people will go to hell, don't tell me I can't do what I feel in any given situation—and don't tell me to go to church.

This coincides with much of what we're hearing from people in the media (the source from where much of this generation is drawing its opinions). Celebrities frequently make statements that support this kind of thinking. In my *Reaching Out to the Unchurched* training workshops, I often share quotes from the media preaching "belief in the spiritual" but resistance to "church or religion."

> "I think I find more strength in faith than I do in organized religion."
>
> - Jon Bon Jovi[xvi]

"I grew up in a family that called itself Catholic. But nobody told me that to pray you have to go to a place. I've always believed in God my own way."

- Actress Penelope Cruz[xvii]

No-way kids don't always have a problem with God. But they're pretty convinced they don't want strict doctrines or church.

The only cure for this resistance to church is a relationship. If my friend Rob's experience is true ("I have never had a student who I built a relationship with say no to church"), then a relationship is the key.

So that brings us back to this question: How are we going to begin a relationship with outreach students?

FIND VENUES FOR FIRST CONTACT

All relationships have a beginning. Think of every student in your group. You met him or her somewhere, probably at your church. That meeting was your first contact with that person. Connecting with the no-way kid begins with first contact.

Sometimes we have no-way kids in our youth groups. Mom made them come or they are visiting with grandma from out of town. They are physically present, but mentally they're wishing they were anywhere else. Regardless of where they are physically, we need to initiate first contact.

Most no-way kids are not going to wander into your youth ministry by choice, so you will have to find a place to meet them— on their turf.

Aaron is a youth worker I know from Toronto. He didn't have contact with any outreach students at all, but he noticed a bunch of kids hanging out at the local skateboard park. So Aaron and his friend Giovanni (another youth pastor at a church in town) went to a skate shop and bought boards. They showed up at the park the next day and began skating with a handful of students. Giovanni had skated before, but it became pretty obvious to these students that Aaron didn't know a skateboard from an ironing board. So Aaron asked a few of them, "I'm new at this. Can you show me the basics?"

Aaron began skating with the students. They actually seemed eager to show him how to ride. As they skated, they engaged in conversation. They asked him why he wanted to skateboard, and Aaron responded honestly, "I'm a youth pastor in the community, and I figured it would be a good idea to get out and meet people." Aaron was real, and the students were okay with that.

Aaron looks at that day as a success—even though after 30 minutes he broke his ankle and had to go to the hospital. (Aaron took one for the team.)

Where are the *no-way kids* in your town?

Connecting with these particular students might require the following:

No-Way Kid Location	Method for First Contact
On-campus	Visit campus, volunteer on campus
At after-school clubs or sports practices	Coach, assistant coach, bring snacks
Attending competitions or sports events	Attend competions or games
At a skateboard park	Go skateboarding
At campus ministries like Young Life/Campus Life	Volunteer for these organizations
Add your own here:	Add your own here:

Let's talk about how to make first contact in these venues. I'll use on-campus visits as an example since that is probably the most commonly used method to meet all three types of *outreach students*. But these methods will work at skate parks and sports events alike. Maybe as I discuss some of these methods, you'll think of other opportunities and venues in your area. Each town and region is going to have its own settings where you can safely meet students. These methods will work on your turf or theirs.

Campus visits can also be pretty difficult when you compare them with coaching, skating, or attending sports events. With coaching and skating, you have another task to concentrate on. Relationships are built as you are occupied with the activity. When you attend sports events, there is a game to watch—a nice distraction if conversation proves difficult. With campus visits it's nothing but you walking and talking with students.

For that reason, I'm going to use the venue of campus visits to teach us these basics of initiating contact with *no-way kids*. If you can approach and talk with any student on campus, you can do most anything.

INITIAL GREETING

I don't know if you'll find this comforting or disturbing, but visiting a junior high or high school campus for the first time terrifies me. Thoughts fly through my head like, "What if they think I'm a big nerd?" (More like, "What if they discover *I truly am* a big nerd?") "What if no one talks to me at all?" or "What if they ask me a question I can't answer?"

Thankfully I've found that once a student starts talking to you, 75 percent of those fears go away. Here are some steps we can take to be better prepared to initiate conversations with teenagers and answer the questions they throw at us.

1. Be Yourself

The first and foremost rule to visiting a campus is this: *Be yourself.* If you're a geek, face it, you're a geek. If you're a jock, face it, geeks hate you. If you're a snob—well, let's not go there.

Don't try to be something you aren't. Don't tilt your hat sideways if that's not what you do. Students have radars for phoniness like you wouldn't believe. Authenticity is huge with them, so just be who you are.

If you're thinking, "Well, I'm not a gregarious person. I don't do well in social situations," don't worry. You don't have to become the life of the party, but you will have to take some steps that might stretch you socially.

The most important thing is that you find a niche that's you. It might be difficult as you are first learning to break the ice in conversation with students, but you'll eventually find a way to feel comfortable being who you are.

2. Be Ready to Answer Questions

The next step we must take before visiting a campus is this: Be ready to answer, "Who are you?" and "Why are you here?"

Every time you visit a new campus, I promise you will hear those words at some point. So don't be caught trying to think of a pithy answer on the spot.

Why is this question so difficult to answer? For some of us, it's difficult because we really are there because we love students and want to share God's love with them. On most campuses, we aren't allowed to talk about God, so that leaves us with "I love students." And responding with that will only get you a bunch of really funny looks.

So be prepared to answer that question.

"Who are you?"

"I'm Chris. I work at the church down the street and help out here on campus every Wednesday."

Be ready for the follow-up question.

"Help out? Help with what?"

Expect students to ask you questions out of skepticism. How will you answer if a student asked you the questions above?

My friend Rob, who I mentioned earlier in the chapter, is amazing to watch on campus—a true expert in the field. For that reason, I'll be using him as an example throughout this chapter. Rob has a bunch of one-liners he uses at the beginning of the year when students ask him questions. If a student asks him, "Who are you?" sometimes he just says, "I'm Rob. Who are you?" That sometimes prompts the student to share his or her name, but it usually elicits a follow-up question. "Yeah—but why are you here?"

Rob has a gold mine of answers to the "Why are you here?" question. Once, a group of students asked him that question, and Rob replied, "I'm his parole officer," pointing at the biggest student in the group, "and I've come to check up on him."

Usually that brings a laugh from the group. And nine times out of 10, the student who he just pointed to will play along. Rob contends that students have an affinity for and like to joke about being bad or a criminal. "It doesn't matter if I've never met the student," Rob explains. "I told him I was his parole officer. For some reason students like that."

If Rob had said, "I'm his choir director," he would *not* have received such a positive response. But students think it's cool to be an ex-con. Most times students will roll with it. Then Rob has an open door to talk with the group and honestly answer the question, "So what's your real job?"

"I'm Rob. I work for Campus Life."

Spend some time brainstorming answers to those two questions. Here are some samples:

WHO ARE YOU?

- I'm Rob, who are you?

- I'm Traci, but I spell it the cool way.

- I'm Andy. I work at the Central Avenue Teen Center down the street.

- I'm Sabrina, and I'm hungry. Is any of the food worth eating here?

WHY ARE YOU HERE?

- Vice Principal Lee asked me to be here. Why are you here?

- I'm here to help out.

- I'm in 7th grade, but I'm just big for my age. (Which will always make them say, "Seriously, why are you here?" So be ready to answer again.)

- Officially, the school likes having an adult presence around to help out. Unofficially, I'm hoping to find someone who wants to play a little basketball.

- I'm a junior high pastor, and the sign out front said "junior high."

3. Be Ready for Them to Try to Shock You

Once, as Rob walked near a table, he heard one of the student's names—*Danny*. Someone from the table saw Rob and asked him the million-dollar question, "Why are you here?" Rob responded, "I'm here to get the dirt on Danny. Tell me what you know."

Rob's answer worked. Immediately students were shouting out, "Oh, I've got stories!"

One girl walked over to the student named Danny and put her arms around him saying, "Oh, Danny isn't that bad. If I were straight, I'd date him."

Be ready for students to try to shock you. Students love to be noticed, and they love to read your reactions, just like the girl at the beginning of the chapter, "If Satan was a female—that's me." *No-way kids* generally want to make us squirm.

Think about the girl who desperately blurted out, "Oh, Danny isn't that bad. If I were straight, I'd date him." What was this girl really saying? (Side note: What a great teachable moment to train your volunteers. Tell your volunteers about this situation and ask them, "What can we learn about this girl from this question?")

This girl was practically screaming, "Notice me!" Her self-esteem was so poor she had to wear her sexuality on her wrist and her forehead.

Who knows what this girl's sexual orientation actually was. But she was obviously searching for something. Moreover, she wanted to see how Rob would react to her declaration.

How would you respond to this girl?

"Burn in hell, sinner!" Hopefully not. Not only would you be ending your campus ministry, but your reaction would be completely opposite from Christ's reaction to those he encountered who were in the depths of sin. I don't know anybody who would actually say those words, but I know plenty who would think it.

Be careful. Students are perceptive. If we show judgment on our faces when students try to shock us, we will close doors to ministry opportunities.

4. Be Ready to Learn Names

The fourth step in preparation for initiating conversations with teenagers is *learning names*. Names are powerful.

When I go on campus, I learn a student's name and use the name the next time I see him; it speaks volumes to that student. Learning names communicates to students you care enough to remember who they are. It transforms an anonymous student to "Michael."

Don't dismiss the discipline of learning names if you feel you're not good at remembering them. My friend Rob—the campus ministry guru—readily admits he's terrible with names. He confessed that when he's done visiting campus, he sits in his car and writes down every single name he can remember with a short description.

Trevor- shy student with blue eyes

Jackie- Goth girl with nose ring

Haley- proclaimed lesbian, long blonde hair

Nathan- big student with big ol' wig

This discipline helps him remember 80 to 90 percent of the students' names the next time he sees them.

Rob has become very good with names. One time the principal and Rob were discussing some situations on campus, and Rob shared what he observed, mentioning numerous students by name. The principal was surprised at Rob's knowledge of the student body. He continued to seek out Rob with questions since Rob seemed to have a thumb on the pulse of the students on campus. It all starts with learning names.

5. Be Ready with Break-the-Ice Questions

On rare occasions, students will just ignore you, and you will have to take the initiative to approach a group of students to break the ice.

Even when students initiate dialogue with you, asking your name or why you are there, eventually an awkward silence will emerge. You'll need to keep the conversation going.

How do you do this?

The best way to initiate contact with a group of students is with a question. But don't barge into a group with a deep question. Start with something light and easy to answer.

So who can tell me what the food is like here? Is there something I should avoid?

That's an easy question to answer. It also makes it fun for the student. Students like to poke fun at stuff they don't like. "Avoid the coleslaw. By all means, avoid the coleslaw."

I also would ask questions that gave students a chance to share their opinion about something they like.

I'm doing a study on teenagers and the music they listen to. What kind of music do you think most students at this school enjoy?

Don't enter into this conversation without a little bit of knowledge. In other words, do your homework if you're going to try this question. I recommend spending time on Billboard.com and iTunes looking at top artists, listening to samples, and taking notice of the most popular artists, songs, and music styles.

I also wouldn't use this question unless I actually was doing this study (as a matter of integrity). Consider what an awesome opportunity this is. As a youth worker, I'm constantly studying the media and trying to stay current with what students are watching and listening to. So this question actually serves two purposes: It helps break the ice, and it teaches me about the specific youth culture I'm trying to reach.

This question can also lead to follow-up questions:

What is your favorite song right now?

Who is your favorite artist?

What would your friends find in your 'most recently played' on your iPod?

And then, if you get comfortable with the crowd, you might try this question.

What song would embarrass you if any of these guys found out you had it on your iPod?

Well-thought-out questions can help you break the ice.

Brainstorm good questions with your team of adult volunteers. This is not only a good exercise to get them thinking about making first contacts; it can provide you with some fantastic ideas for these situations as well. (I've also provided a brief list of some additional questions in the appendix.)

6. Don't Cling to Christian Students

The final step in being prepared to initiate conversations with teenagers is more of a "reminder" than an actual "step." The reminder is simple: *Talk to outreach students.*

We want to connect with *all six types* of students. Most of us already have relationships with Christian students. This is great. I'll focus on our ministry to these students in chapters eight, nine, and 10. Meeting Christian students on campus is fantastic. We can be a great encouragement to these students in a place that can be a very discouraging environment. But at the same time, we don't want to miss the opportunity to meet and connect with *outreach students.* If we build relationships with a few *outreach students,* they will help us connect with other *outreach students.*

One day, while talking with a bunch of *outreach students* he'd built relationships with, Cody introduced Rob to a senior named Matt. Cody was excited to tell Matt all about Rob. "He's the coolest adult you'll ever meet. He's helped me through a bunch of my problems."

Matt whipped out his cell phone and started typing. Then he looked up at Rob. "Can I have your phone number?"

"Sure." Rob replied, giving Matt the number.

Matt punched the number in his phone. "I put you under 'HELP.'"

Cody's endorsement was all Matt needed to hear. *Outreach students* open the doors to ministry with other *outreach students.*

When I first started campus ministry, I only knew one student—an *outreach student.* She introduced me to all her friends—*outreach students.* Pretty soon, I knew a huge number of students at this particular school.

One day I met with a local pastor who happened to bring his daughter along with him to our meeting. I quickly discovered she went to the school I visited regularly, and I began asking her about some of the students I knew. As I listed a bunch of names, her dad asked her, "Haley, do you know any of these students?"

Haley had a horrified look on her face. She clicked her tongue, "Yeah... they're all troublemakers."

I've observed this phenomenon time and time again: Very often, our Christian students don't like it when we reach out to the "notorious sinners" of the campus.

Such was the ministry of Jesus. Jesus spent time with believers and nonbelievers. Some of the religious folk of the day weren't excited about his ministry to the sinners, but Jesus still hung out with both groups. He spent time in the synagogues with people who wanted to learn about the Hebrew Scriptures, and at other times he hung out with notorious sinners. When the religious leaders of the day tried to confront him about his time spent with sinners, Jesus responded, "Healthy people don't need a doctor—sick people do." Then he went on to say, "For I have come to call not those who think they are righteous, but those who know they are sinners" (Mathew 9:12-13 NLT).

The initial greeting stage is the most difficult part of making first contact. Once you break the ice, learn a few names, and have one conversation with a student, the next conversations will be easier.

Remember:

1. Be yourself.

2. Be ready for their questions.

3. Be ready for their attempts to shock you.

4. Try your best to get their names and commit them to memory.

5. Have a few questions handy to help you break the ice if necessary.

6. Don't favor *discipleship students* when you're on campus.

Developing a Relationship

After my initial encounters with students, my goals are relationship building and information gathering. I become a listener, not a talker; I want to hear rather than be heard. As I develop these relationships, my next steps are to:

- Look for common ground in conversation

- Create opportunities to connect *one-on-one*

I'll go into more detail about both of these steps in the next chapter.

GOALS

As you are connecting with students for the first time, you might not know where they fall in our *six-types-of-students* table right away. It might take several conversations before you discover the student is even an *outreach student*. You may get to know a smart-mouthed, rebellious teen and assume he's a *no-way kid*, only to eventually find out he's just the pastor's son.

My main goal is always to help students move to the right on the *six-types-of-students* table. Therefore, my main goal for the *no-way kid* is that they would become willing to check things out. Relationships help change *no-way kids* into *checking-things-out kids*.

SIX TYPES OF STUDENTS

Outreach			Discipleship		
No Way	Not Interested	Checking Things Out	Stagnant	Growing	Looking for Ministry
Tyler ————————————→ Tyler					

Remember, *no-way kids* are, by definition, against the idea of church and are sometimes against God. They may be aggressive toward you initially; they may even try to shock you. But don't get caught arguing with them—just love them. As you build relationships with *no-way kids*, their walls will start to collapse.

The older the students, the more they may actually want to engage in spiritual discussions. College *no-way kids* are more prone to want to debate with you about key objections they might have about Christianity, Christians, and the church. If you work with older teenagers and college students, you may want to prepare for these conversations. But keep them as respectful discussions as opposed to heated debates. (Again, Dan Kimball's book, *They Like Jesus, But Not the Church*[xviii], is a fantastic resource to equip you for these conversations.)

In my personal ministry with middle and high school students, I almost never engage in debates. I found most students use them as excuses for the real objection—*they don't want to change the way they live their lives*. Furthermore, I achieved much better results just being a friend. This opened the door to very comfortable and real spiritual discussions where I was given the opportunity to share the truth of the gospel. (I lay out that entire process step by step in my book *Do They Run When They See You Coming?*[xix])

6
ONE-ON-ONE WITH THE *NOT-INTERESTED KID*

	Outreach		Discipleship		
No Way	Not Interested	Checking Things Out	Stagnant	Growing	Looking for Ministry

DESCRIPTION:

The *not-interested kid* is probably most common kid we will find on a school campus. Most often they don't attend church; not because they have anything against God or the Bible, they just would rather be— *anywhere else.* They are simply *not interested.*

OUR GOALS WITH THE *NOT-INTERESTED KID:*

Our goals with *not-interested kids* are identical to our goals with *no-way kids.* We want to befriend them, listen to them, and try to earn their trust. Once we build relationships, we hope they will become willing to *check things out* (engage in spiritual conversations, visit a venue where those conversations happen, or visit a place where they can hear spiritual truths).

My friend KJ is a youth director in a large church. One day he received a phone call from a parent pleading with him to help her with her son, Ryan.

Ryan had been getting in some trouble at school and at home. The afternoon prior, Ryan's dad had come home from work a little early, only to find Ryan and his buddies smoking pot in the back yard. After their initial reactions, Ryan's parents sat him down to try to search for a cause behind symptoms that had recently been surfacing. When they drilled Ryan about why he was acting out, he simply responded, "Because I just don't care."

Distraught, Ryan's mom begged KJ for advice. After talking with KJ for about half an hour, she asked him, "Is there anything you can do?" KJ agreed to meet with Ryan.

Two days later KJ sat across the table from Ryan at a local burger joint. Ryan's hands were crossed in front of him as he stared at his fries. KJ began asking light questions about school and home.

"Tell me about your school."

"What is your favorite part of school?"

"What is your least favorite part?"

"What do you like to do when you're not at school?"

Ryan began to relax a little with each question. He liked talking about his interests. KJ got the feeling not many people had listened to Ryan. The more Ryan got the opportunity to talk, the more comfortable he seemed.

KJ continued, "Tell me about home."

This question made Ryan twitch in his seat, but he didn't hold back.

"Do you know what my parents' problem is?" Ryan began to unload his feelings. KJ sat there and listened for what seemed like 10 minutes without Ryan taking a breath. Finally Ryan blurted out, "... and they keep making me go to church." Ryan stopped short and looked at KJ, wondering if he'd said too much.

KJ didn't flinch. He quickly came to Ryan's defense and said, "I wasn't always a big fan of church, either." Ryan exhaled. *Whew.*

KJ asked, "Tell me what you think of church when you go."

Ryan thought for a minute, and then he began to share. "Church is fine for some people, just not for me." Ryan talked about some of the hypocrisy he saw, he named a few students he saw at church who he didn't think belonged in church, and then he shared some frustrations with church in general.

KJ let him talk. A few times KJ interjected, identifying with some of Ryan's feelings, and relating them to similar frustrations KJ had experienced.

As time passed, KJ realized Ryan really didn't have anything against church. He just didn't find it relevant to his interests at all. This is characteristic of *not-interested kids.*

After an hour and a half, KJ concluded, "It sounds like you think church is pretty boring. You're also experiencing some of the doubts and frustrations many people experience with church; I know I have. But you also seem to be searching for answers in some of the wrong places. I think you're bright enough to know that. You just haven't chosen to act on that knowledge yet. I hope you do, sooner, rather than later."

KJ left it at that. They laughed and talked a little more about sports and movies. KJ paid the bill and thanked Ryan for his time. As KJ got in his car, he wondered whether his time with Ryan had been effective. Nonverbal cues don't always speak volumes. KJ had definitely noticed Ryan liked having someone to talk to, but he didn't know if their time together had accomplished anything.

Later that night KJ received a call from Ryan's mom. "Ryan really enjoyed his time with you."

"He did?" KJ asked honestly. "I didn't know."

Ryan's mom asked KJ if he could spend more time with Ryan. KJ knew he didn't have time to add another student to his weekly one-on-one schedule. He was already meeting individually with six students in his small group regularly. But KJ told Ryan's mom, "I have a person who I want to introduce Ryan to."

KJ had an intern named Tom. Tom had a rough background himself and was drawn to students like Ryan. KJ took them both out for a milkshake and introduced them. The three of them talked, and at the end of their time, Tom asked Ryan if he'd like to get together again. Ryan agreed. *The handoff was successful.*

KJ talked with Tom later that day and gave him clear goals. "Love this student and give him a chance to heal from these wounds. Ryan is tired of church, and he feels a little bit burned by church people. He needs to see something authentic."

KJ went on, "Secondly, find out where Ryan is spiritually. Ryan has been raised being forced to go to church, but I don't know if he's ever really put his trust in Jesus. Finally, as he grows more comfortable with you, invite him to youth group with you some Wednesday night. Make plans for dinner beforehand, and then introduce him to some of the guys." KJ gave him a few suggestions of guys whom he thought Ryan would mesh with. "Let him experience your small group."

Tom began investing in Ryan, caring for him, and listening to him. Several times spiritual topics came up, and Tom listened to Ryan. It was obvious Ryan was interested in running his own life, but he was slowly becoming receptive to talking about salvation.

Eventually Ryan began coming to church with Tom and was open to learning more.

I can't tell you the end of the story because that's where the story ends right now—it's a journey in progress. This process takes time; and it has in this case. So far, it's been three months from the first phone call KJ received from Ryan's mom. But *one-on-one* attention has already helped change a *not-interested kid* into a *checking-things-out kid*.

He used to be forced to go to church, but now he goes because he enjoys the relationships there, and he is open to spiritual conversations.

SIX TYPES OF STUDENTS

Outreach			Discipleship		
No Way	Not Interested	Checking Things Out	Stagnant	Growing	Looking for Ministry
	Ryan ⟶ Ryan				

It all started with dinner at a greasy burger joint.

GO TO THEM

Not-interested kids aren't typically in our youth groups. If they have a choice in the matter, they will be anywhere *but* church. Maybe they've been to church a couple times and thought it was boring. In their minds, they've *got way better things to do than church*. That's why we usually need to go to them. Like the *no-way kids*, they don't want to come to our programs.

In a recent Junior High Pastor's Summit sponsored by Youth Specialties, Mark Oestricher said, "We need to look at the existing social networks of students. Instead of trying to attract them with our stuff, we should go to where these networks already are and connect with them there."

Mark is right, especially if we're talking about *no-way* and *not-interested kids*. We need to stop putting all our efforts into drawing students to our programs. I'm not saying we shouldn't ever do outreach programs or events; I believe an outreach event can be *one* of many effective tools to reach *checking-things-out kids* (we'll talk about that in the next chapter). Not to mention, once we build relationships with *no-way* and *not-interested kids*, these events can be good opportunities. But outreach events tend to be ineffective in reaching *not-interested kids* if we don't already have relationships with them.

Yet many youth ministries focus 99 percent of their outreach efforts on inviting students to their programs. No wonder we're missing *not-interested kids*; they, by definition, are *not interested* in our programs.

THE TYPICAL STUDENT

A few years ago I got the chance to interview the young actress Hayden Panettiere (most popular from her role as "the cheerleader" on TV's *Heroes*). Hayden sounded like a typical *not-interested kid*.

When I asked Hayden about church, this was her response.

"I don't go to church that often. I go for like Easter Sunday. There is such a short period of time to live, and I'd rather spend it 'living life' as opposed to sitting down and praying."[xx]

If you visit your local campus, this is by far the largest category of students you'll encounter. When I worked with *Youth for Christ* reaching a local junior high campus, we frequently invited students to church with us. Initially, over 50 percent of them refused. None of them seemed to have anything against church; they just didn't have any interest in giving up their Sunday mornings. Whenever

I invited students, I could almost see some of them weighing it in their minds, *"Hmmmmm. Sleep in, lay around the couch and watch TV... or get up early, dress up in uncomfortable clothes, and be bored out of my mind by some preacher."*

Typically, church will lose out to laziness and misconceptions.

How do you reach these kinds of students? *Relationships.* Most students won't give church a try without a relationship. But once a student trusts you, he'll try anything—*once.*

THAT INITIAL CONNECTION

Some of you might wonder, "How do I start a relationship with a *not-interested kid*?"

That's a great question. And the answer isn't that far from the approach we use with *no-way kids.* If anything, *not-interested kids* should be a little easier to talk with than *no-way kids* because they tend to be a little less hostile toward the church and people in ministry.

Much of what we do in the beginning of any relationship involves finding common ground. If you are coaching, sports is great common ground: You like football, they like football. If you're tutoring, academics is the common ground; they need help with math, you're good at math. If you're a computer whiz, then stop by the computer center. Many schools need volunteers to monitor their computer labs. These are all good starting points for relationships.

I remember looking for common ground when I invited a *not-interested kid* out to our campus ministry on a Wednesday night. Kenny was an incredible basketball player and easily one of the most popular students on campus. When another student introduced me to Kenny, I asked him questions in order to discover common ground.

"So, I hear you're quite a basketball player."

"Uh-huh."

"You play on the school team?"

"Uh-huh."

"You're pretty tall—are you a forward?"

"Uh-huh."

"Who's your favorite player?"

"Kobe."

"Ever been to one of his games?"

"Nope."

"Do you know Kobe speaks three languages?"

He paused at this question, "Really?"

It took me six questions before I really got his attention. So I tried one more.

"Do you ever play basketball during lunch?"

"Yeah."

And that's all I needed to know. I love lunchtime basketball games (even though I am barely good enough to keep up with junior highers). And I found my common ground—basketball.

A couple weeks went by and I always made an effort to say, "Hi," to Kenny. Sometimes it was just, "Hi." Other times it was a little about the Lakers or the incredible number of points Kobe Byant had scored the night before.

One day I found two basketballs and asked Kenny and a couple of others if they wanted to play. Ten minutes later we were in the middle of a game of knockout. (Knockout is a basketball game like "21" or "Horse.") Kenny usually cleaned house.

As I got to know Kenny better, I invited him to our Wednesday night on-campus activity. Kenny wasn't interested, so I didn't push it.

One day I was doing pretty well in a game of knockout. We were tied, and Kenny was pretty sure he was going to beat us all, as usual. But this time I decided to make a bet.

"Kenny, I'll bet you I can beat you this time."

Kenny laughed. "Sure—I'll take your money. What do you want to bet?"

"If you win, I have to take you and all the other guys here out for fast food of your choice after school today."

They all cheered and started giving each other high fives—prematurely, of course.

I continued, "But if I win, then you have to come to Campus Life tomorrow night."

Kenny didn't even hesitate. I could tell it wasn't much of a risk for him anyway. In the past he'd already declined going to Campus Life, but he knew a bunch of friends who attended. How bad could it be?

The game was on.

This was a win-win for me. If I lost, I got to take every one of these students out for fast food and get to know them better. If I lost, Kenny was coming Wednesday night.

I "knocked" Kenny out in less than three minutes that day. (God must have been involved!) Kenny came to Campus Life and had a great time. Two months later Kenny accepted Christ. I ended up discipling Kenny and one of his friends who also put his trust in Jesus.

It all started with finding common ground.

ONE-ON-ONE VERSUS ONE-ON-SIX

I used the exact same idea a couple of years later at my church. I was working with the junior high group at the time, and one of the students began inviting a bunch of his friends to swim parties during the week. These friends were typical *not-interested kids*. They came out to the swim parties but weren't interested in anything churchy. (If these students were believers, I'd have called them *stagnant kids*. But these students didn't know Christ at all, and they weren't willing to give church a try.)

I tried the basketball bet with these guys and lost. No worries— the next week I took them all out for fast food together.

Six students at a fast-food joint is a much different experience than one student at a fast-food joint. Taking six students is like leading a small group. Worse yet, they aren't even on your territory. So when they start acting up (which six junior high boys tend to do), there's not much you can do about it.

Tonya, a youth worker who has used our ministry's resources for years, wrote me about a time she invited a student out to dinner. The student asked if her friends could come. Even though Tonya really just wanted some *one-on-one* time, she agreed.

What Tonya described was a long, painful evening of the three students running all over the restaurant, ignoring her, joking with each other, and being completely disrespectful. *One-on-one*, the same student might have opened up. But around her friends she proved very difficult to talk with.

Tonya and I both learned the importance of *one-on-one* from our experiences. If you ask a student to lunch or dinner, aim for one-on-one time—one-on-two maximum. Two students are easy to handle, but three or more becomes more difficult.

If a student asks to bring a friend, simply respond, "We'll have plenty of opportunities to hang out as a group. I really just want to hear from you."

Yes, some students might be intimidated by this. That's why I always make sure to meet in a very public place. Also, I always try to meet the student's parent(s) first. (We'll spend a lot of time talking about these kinds of precautions and boundaries in chapter 13.)

Focusing on Our Goals

With *no-way kids* and *not-interested kids* we need to—

- Learn about their cultures, attitudes, and trends

- Find out where they hang out in our communities

- Discover venues where we can make first contacts with them

- Learn names and interests

- Ask well-placed questions and listen carefully

- Find common ground

- Create opportunities to try to connect with them *one-on-one*

Remember: Relationships can change *not-interested kids* into *checking-things-out kids*.

THE INVESTMENT OF TIME

This process takes time because building relationships takes time.

A youth worker named John shared with me about his investment in a student named Andrew.

The first time Andrew looked into my eyes, he was holding a knife to my stomach.

Andrew was a student who slept all day long through

my class. He never lifted his head. He was new. It was the middle of the school year, and he was moved to our private school because no other would take him.

Day after day Andrew would walk into my class, put his head down, and never pick it up the rest of the day. I tried waking him, but he'd just lie there, regardless of how much I tugged on his jacket. After numerous attempts to wake him and notifcation of the administrator, Andrew was suspended for two days.

As I was walking to my car that day, Andrew stepped around the corner with a knife. Leaning in really closely, he told me if I touched his jacket again he'd kill me.

I'm not sure why, but I laughed and said, "Man, people getting killed over the school uniform jackets now? What has this world come to? It's not even a Nike jacket."

He wanted to laugh, but didn't.

Two weeks passed, and I did not hear a word from Andrew. Then, out of the blue, he came to me and asked for something to do. We gave him the placement test, and he punched the computer in anger. Andrew could not put his name in the computer because he didn't know how to spell his last name. It was then we discovered Andrew did not know how to read or write. He was 15 years old.

I offered to stay after school and tutor him for reading.

Miraculously, he accepted.

Day after day I met with Andrew. It was awkward at first, but he slowly began to open up. Over time, this led to conversations about my relationship with Christ and my other job as a youth pastor.

Time passed. I invited Andrew to youth group one night, and he came with his gang. That night, three students put their trust in Jesus, including Andrew.

We continued to meet after school in the library to study words and the Word. When I left that school, Andrew was 18, could read at a tenth-grade level, and was leading Bible studies at the school. He is now in tech school learning to be an auto mechanic. He teaches youth at a local Spanish church as well.

We live in a day where we want quick solutions and quick results. Most of the results take time. In Andrew's case, it took a year to get him to trust me, a year before he trusted Jesus, and he now has a lifetime of growth ahead in his relationship with Jesus.

Transformation takes time; we must be committed to investing in students for the long haul.

DESCRIPTION:

7

ONE-ON-ONE WITH THE CHECKING-THINGS-OUT KID

Outreach			Discipleship		
No Way	Not Interested	Checking Things Out	Stagnant	Growing	Looking for Ministry

Checking-things-out kids are willing and open to engage in spiritual conversations and visiting places where those conversations happen. They often recognize voids in their lives and are in search for answers—that's why they are open to *checking things out.*

OUR GOALS WITH THE *CHECKING-THINGS-OUT KID:*

Our goals with *checking-things-out kids* are to build relationships with them, care for their felt needs, and expose them to the gospel message.

Zacchaeus was a wee little man,

A wee little man was he.

He climbed up in that Sycamore tree,

Mmmm ... da... da.... da... hmmm.... so he could

see. (I always forget that line.)

If you grew up in church, you might remember the song and story about Zacchaeus. I love this story because it gives us a true glimpse of Jesus by demonstrating the way he treated those who were difficult to love.

In the last two chapters we've discovered how vital it is for us to go outside the church walls to engage with *outreach kids*. As we've explored what this process looks like, one of the goals I've repeated several times is to *create opportunities to connect with them one-on-one.* Maybe that's as simple as inviting someone to dinner.

Jesus shows us a perfect example of engaging with someone one-one-one in the story of Zacchaeus in Luke 19:

> Jesus entered Jericho and was passing through. A man was there by the name of Zacchaeus; he was a chief tax collector and was wealthy. He wanted to see who Jesus was, but because he was short he could not see over the crowd. So he ran ahead and climbed a sycamore-fig tree to see him, since Jesus was coming that way.
>
> When Jesus reached the spot, he looked up and said to him, "Zacchaeus, come down immediately. I must stay at your house today." So he came down at once and

welcomed him gladly.

All the people saw this and began to mutter, "He has gone to be the guest of a sinner."

But Zacchaeus stood up and said to the Lord, "Look, Lord! Here and now I give half of my possessions to the poor, and if I have cheated anybody out of anything, I will pay back four times the amount."

Jesus said to him, "Today salvation has come to this house, because this man, too, is a son of Abraham. For the Son of Man came to seek and to save what was lost." (Luke 19:1-10)

Let's look at what is happening in this story:

- Zacchaeus is not only a sinner; he has a *reputation* of a sinner. It is public information that this guy is bad news.

- Zacchaeus is a *checking-things-out guy*. He "wanted to see who Jesus was." We find out later in the story that this guy was most likely searching for forgiveness and meaning.

- It appears as if God's people weren't reaching out to this guy. If anything, they were ignoring him or turning him away.

- Jesus didn't worry about what anyone else thought. Instead, he announced publicly he'd connect with him *one-on-one*. "I must stay at your house today."

Jesus exemplifies the power of relational connection. Jesus is in a crowd of people and recognizes Zacchaeus' need for one-on-one attention. That simple act of just *noticing* Zacchaeus was the key to this tax collector's transformation.

Is there a *checking-things-out kid* you know who is dying to be noticed? Maybe no one has ever taken the time to listen and hear his or her struggles. No one has engaged in spiritual conversations. Perhaps no one has even offered an invitation to church.

The student may be open to all of this—if someone would just notice.

WILLING TO "CHECK THINGS OUT"

Amy had multiple mental and emotional problems, drug and alcohol addictions, and struggles with weight. A youth worker I know named Laura met Amy at a skate park during a youth group manhunt (a scavenger hunt using people instead of things). Laura walked up to Amy and asked her what she was doing. Amy said, "Nothing much—just standing here asking God to send me some friends."

Amy never had a mother in her life, was raised by an alcoholic father, and was never taught how to care for herself properly. Laura began to spend one-on-one time with her, listening to her and being a friend.

One night Laura had a girls' night at her house with some of the youth group and included Amy. When Amy arrived and took off her shoes, the smell just about knocked everyone over. Rather than reacting or giving her a hard time about it, Laura decided to give her a pedicure—what Laura later called "the modern version of foot washing." Amy had never experienced anything like it and was an immediate fan.

During the pedicure, Laura listened to Amy describe some of the pain of growing up without a mother. As they talked, Laura was able to introduce the idea of taking care of themselves as godly women. From then on, each time Amy came over she'd say, "Hey! Let's do pedicures." And they usually did.

Even before Laura met Amy, she was open and willing to let God change her. All it took was Laura's gift of friendship and acceptance of Amy into her life.

When Amy introduced her sister Nikki to Laura, Nikki immediately announced she was a Buddhist. So Laura invited her over to the next girls' night along with Amy. That night Nikki began to ask spiritual questions. Laura and Nikki had a long talk about the differences between Buddhism and Christianity. Soon both girls were attending every youth meeting and even began studying the Bible and praying. It wasn't long before Amy put her trust in Christ. Soon after, Nikki also decided to put her trust in Christ at an evening Bible study. Relational ministry is a powerful tool.

A professional youth counselor recently told me, "The mentor is the first unconditional adult in a troubled client's life." We might be the first adult in a student's life who isn't barking at them, "Clean your room," or "Where is your homework?" We have an opportunity to hang out with a student for the simple reason that *we care*.

It's amazing when you think about the results of Laura's unconditional love. Amy was a *checking-things-out kid*. She craved friendship and was searching for fulfillment. Her sister Nikki was a *no-way kid*. But, being sisters with Amy, she was willing to engage in some conversation with Laura. Once Laura established trust, Nikki was willing to "check things out," too. Because of Laura's relational investment, Nikki moved from a *no-way kid* to a *checking-things-out kid*. Then both sisters trusted Jesus and moved on to becoming *growing kids*.

SIX TYPES OF STUDENTS

Outreach			Discipleship		
No Way	Not Interested	Checking Things Out	Stagnant	Growing	Looking for Ministry
Nikki ——————————→		Nikki ———————		→ Nikki	
		Amy ———————		→ Amy	

Notice Nikki skipped columns, bypassing *Not Interested* and graduating straight to *Checking Things Out*. Both skipped over *Stagnant*. Skipping stages is actually common—and desired. When *outreach students* become *discipleship students*, we should always begin discipling them and get them plugged into the rest of the church family.

CREATING A PLACE TO BELONG

Today's young people are looking for a place of *belonging*. Many of them don't find belonging at school or even at home. As teens grow more independent, they become less involved in sports and other activities and retreat to the Internet in search of connection. But, as we explored in chapter one, this is leaving them with fewer close friends and void of face-to-face relationships.

Many *checking-things-out kids* we encounter are looking for relationships to fill that void. They are in search of places where they can belong.

We can provide these venues, places where they can connect, build meaningful relationships, talk about relevant issues, and safely engage in spiritual conversations. The venues are often created by our—dare I say—*programming*. (I sometimes avoid the word *programming* since some people consider programs to be numbers-focused or shallow.)

Sometimes we can even offer different types of venues, meeting different needs. A youth worker in my city provides a fun Monday-night hang-out time at a local teen center where he is able to build relationships with hundreds of students. But he also offers a Thursday morning breakfast club where students show up in a side room at a local restaurant for breakfast, engaging in deeper conversations with adults at each table. This five-dollar breakfast (always free for first timers) attracts more than 20 students a week who love the sense of belonging and the safe arena to talk about relevant issues in their lives.

"I'D LIKE TO TALK MORE ABOUT THIS"

When we get a *checking-things-out kid* to attend church on a regular basis, we have the tendency to assume we're done. But how do we know if he's getting his questions answered?

That's where one-on-one time comes in. Let me introduce you to a helpful little tool called the "I'd Like to Talk More about This" checkbox.

At the end of your program—your campus outreach, youth program, or even your Bible study—hand out a card to everyone attending. Ask them to write their names and phone numbers on the cards. Then ask them to write "I'd like to talk more about this" and draw a check box next to it. Announce, "If you check that box, one of us will take you out for ice cream in the next week."

For my group, I actually made little cards we called "React Cards." They looked something like this: (I also included one of these in the appendix for you to copy easily.)

MY REACTION

Name: _____

Phone: _____ (cell? home?)

☐　I enjoyed tonight's topic.

☐　I'd like to talk more about this...

☐　Why lie? I'd just like someone to take me to ice cream!

Comments: _____

_____

I used these cards all the time with my campus ministry, letting students know we love to hear feedback from them. Each week we would receive cards from a handful of students who checked the box, *I'd like to talk more about this*. And each week we'd have some students check, *Why lie? I'd just like someone to take me to ice cream*. Regardless of what they checked, we got a chance to hang out with them one-on-one that week.

My team of adult leaders would get together at the end of the night, and I'd distribute these response cards, asking, "Who would like to meet with Curtis?"

My adult leaders, especially the shy ones, loved the React Cards because it made connecting with students a lot easier to initiate.

ONE-ON-ONE MEETINGS

Some of you might be wondering what you do at one of these one-on-one meetings with a *checking-things-out kid*. The short answer is: Listen, show genuine care, and look for opportunities to share Christ.

Listen

In chapter three I touched on the intentions debate. On one hand we have people who share Christ by all means necessary. They are quick to offend because they don't appear to care for people's needs; they just want to convert them.

One of the major mistakes this group makes is not listening. If a *checking-things-out kid* is pouring her heart out about frustrations, she doesn't want to hear, "If you died tonight, appeared before the gates of heaven, and God asked you, 'Why should I let you into my heaven?' what would you say?" That would be ridiculous.

So listen to felt needs, but don't stop at listening...

Care for felt needs

If a student shares a struggle with math, help with math. If you stink at math (like I do), then I'll bet you can help find a tutor.

Jesus didn't walk up to hungry people and say, "Quit your whining. You need salvation, not food." He fed them. Sometimes he'd even use that miracle as an opportunity to talk about a relationship with God.

Take a look at John 6. Jesus fed more than 5,000 people. Amazing, huh? But don't stop reading there. Many of those people followed Jesus to the other side of the lake (where Jesus took a short cut—across the lake). There, Jesus basically said to them, "Some of you are just here for the food. Why don't you stop seeking temporary stuff like food and start seeking the eternal life I can give you?"

As we spend time with students, we need to care about them holistically. Sometimes they will just want somebody to listen. Other times they might be looking for answers. Be sensitive to them. As time passes and you build relationships with them, meeting some of their physical and emotional needs, you'll encounter opportunities to share Christ with them, meeting their spiritual needs as well.

As important as meeting student needs is, we must not stop there. Recently this topic came up with my friend Greg Stier in an interview for our ministry's podcast. We were discussing social justice and its tendency to omit the gospel message. Many churches have become good at reaching out to the community and feeding the poor, but they skip sharing the truth of the gospel.

Greg spoke out against social justice without the gospel message. He said, "I love feeding the poor. Heck, I was the poor. But if we just feed people and don't share God's truth, we're gonna just have a bunch of people in hell with full stomachs."

Anyone close to Greg knows how much he cares for people. Greg's compassion for them doesn't end at feeding them or meeting their physical needs. Greg is passionate about sharing the truth of the gospel with them. Jesus did the same. We need to follow his example.

So how do we get from meeting students' needs to talking with them about the gospel?

Look for opportunities to share Christ

My biggest fear going into a one-on-one appointment was, "What if we have nothing to talk about?"

When I began in ministry, I asked my friend Leonard about this fear. Leonard told me, "Just be prepared with a bunch of questions."

Over the years I learned one-on-one appointments became easier as I mastered the use of well-placed questions.

When you first sit down with a student at a one-on-one appointment, the conversation should start pretty lightly.

> What food do you usually order when you come to this place?
>
> If you were allowed to order anything on the menu—as much as you wanted—what would you order?
>
> What is your favorite place to eat?
>
> If you could take one person who you know to dinner, who would that be?

As both of you become more comfortable, you'll be able to dive a little deeper. I'd use "digging-deeper" questions to help me transition to a deeper conversation. These aren't questions like, "If you died tonight..." They're just fun questions that can sometimes help transition from talking about fast food or baseball to something a little deeper.

Here's a few I like:

DIGGING-DEEPER QUESTIONS

If they made a movie of your life, who would you want to play you? Why?

If you could visit any place in the world, where would you go and why? Who would you bring with you?

What's one job you might like when you grow up? Why?

When you were little, who did you most often imagine yourself as?

Who do you admire most? What do you admire?

If you were going to create a hero today, what qualities would you give? Do you know anybody close to that?

What is your number one goal in life right now? What are you doing that will get you there? What are you doing that will take you away from this goal?

What could you do right now to improve your life?

What is one item in your house you should really throw

out but probably never will?

"Digging-deeper" questions can help us segue from casual to something a little deeper. As we dive deeper, opportunities will arise to share about Jesus.

You can probably see how many of these questions are open doors to bringing up the gospel message. A transition from these questions to the gospel is sometimes as easy as saying, "Can I share something with you?"

Ask permission to share the gospel. If they give you permission, share what Jesus has done for you and the relationship he offers them through faith.

Many of you might like more specifics on how to share the gospel message. If you have more questions about these conversations and how to share Jesus, I encourage you to read some books specifically about evangelism. I love Greg Stier's book *Dare 2 Share: A Field Guide to Sharing Your Faith*.[xxi] If you want to know more about how to create opportunities to talk about Jesus and share the gospel specifically with an *outreach student*, I encourage you to read my book *Do They Run When They See You Coming: Reaching Out to Unchurched Teenagers*.[xxii]

In the next chapter we'll take a closer look at what this entire process looks like, including sharing the gospel.

8

WHAT CONNECTING WITH *OUTREACH STUDENTS* LOOKS LIKE

PICTURE OF THE PROCESS

Outreach			Discipleship		
No Way	Not Interested	Checking Things Out	Stagnant	Growing	Looking for Ministry

In the three *outreach student* chapters, we reviewed some of the basics when it comes to connecting with them:

- Learn about their cultures, attitudes, and trends

- Find out where they hang out in our communities

- Discover venues where we can make first contacts with them

- Learn names and interests

- Ask well-placed questions and listen carefully
- Find common ground
- Create opportunities to try to connect with them *one-on-one*

Our goal with all three types of *outreach students* is to get one-on-one. Through one-on-one conversations we build deeper relationships that can open doors to sharing Christ.

PUTTING IT ALL INTO PRACTICE

Let's look at an example of what this whole process of connecting with *outreach students* might actually look like.

Tyler was a brand-new youth minister, excited to get started at his first church. One of his first goals was to gain a better understanding of the youth culture in his area. In his first few months Tyler invested a lot of time with families who had teens in his church. He built some great relationships with both parents and students.

Right away, Tyler realized he needed to spend time educating himself about the world in which his students lived. First, he read a book on unchurched students and some current online articles about youth culture. These resources helped him have a better sense of the ways in which pop culture was influencing his community.

He subscribed to a weekly youth culture RSS news feed and two blogs to help stay current. He also checked out www.billboard.com and www.MTV.com to see who his students' favorite music artists were and watched a few of the most popular videos.

The next week at youth group, Tyler asked a few high school students he was connected with about the most popular music students listened to at school. The bands they mentioned could've been taken right from the online charts he'd visited earlier that week.

After youth group, Tyler and Jim, a youth volunteer, logged onto a popular social network site (they did this together for accountability and safety), browsing the profiles of teenagers in their area. As they read profiles of local high school students together, they took note of favorite songs and movies, and more importantly, the subjects these students were talking about. Both Jim and Tyler were shocked at the language students used and how vulnerable they were for all to see.

Tyler chose to not use the social network site to contact students, just to observe and learn. His pastor told him they had a situation in town where an online predator tried to meet with a student, so Tyler thought it was wise to avoid any appearance of this kind of evil.

In the first few months of working at the church, Tyler started to investigate where students hung out in his community. His church was in a small town, so after school most students were either home, in sports, at the coffee house on Main Street, or at the Friday-night game. It became obvious to Tyler those Friday-night games were important to everyone in town.

As Tyler started attending games, one of the church members introduced him to the high school principal. She didn't go to church, but she valued adult participation at the school. A few months later, the principal granted Tyler permission to be on campus during lunch. In order to be allowed this privilege, Tyler agreed not to talk about God or "recruit" students to church, but to focus on being a positive adult presence.

On his first visit to the campus, Tyler was filled with anxiety. Thankfully, he saw a few of his students from church, and they made him feel welcome. After spending some time talking with them in the cafeteria, he sensed God wanted him to try to meet some other students.

As Tyler headed into the commons area, he noticed different groups spread across the campus. He finally decided to wander over to a table by the snack bar area where some young boys, probably freshmen, seemed to be eating a variety of junk food.

As Tyler looked up at the snack bar menu he said, "Okay, I see you guys eating nachos, something that looks like a milkshake, and an apple pie. At the football games, I go for the nachos, but here...I don't know. Who can fill me in on what's worth eating at this snack bar?"

Some of the students stared. But the student eating the nachos happily responded, "Oh, trust me. These nachos are the same ones as the game. But they actually put on more cheese here."

The student next to him chimed in, "That's only if you go to Jessica. She puts on double scoops of cheese."

"So does Cody," the first student responded. He looked at Tyler again. "Either line here is safe. Just don't get the old lady on Friday nights. She's stingy with the cheese."

Tyler smiled, "Thanks! You guys are awesome."

After buying nachos (verifying that Cody does indeed provide two scoops of nacho cheese), he returned to the table. "Mind if I sit here?"

The nachos student spoke up again, "Okay."

One of the other students asked Tyler the all-important question, "Who are you?"

"I work for Velveeta," he said, in a tough-guy voice. "I go around schools checking snack bars to see if they provide enough scoops of our cheese on nachos."

"Velveeta doesn't even make nacho cheese," the nachos student retorted.

"Crud. You caught me," Tyler confessed. "I'm really just a local youth pastor who helps out here on campus."

The table got a little bit quiet.

"But I do like nachos," Tyler added. "And that counts for something."

A couple of the students cracked a smile.

"Thanks, by the way," he added quickly, addressing the nachos student. "These nachos are good. Should I just call you 'Nacho' from now on?"

Nacho smiled, "I've been called worse."

Tyler continued the small talk for a few minutes as he finished his nachos. After asking some light questions to the guys around the table (like the "break-the-ice" questions in chapter five), Tyler brought up the Friday-night games. He found out most of the guys attended the games, but none of them played football. Three of the guys ran track; the others didn't participate in sports at all. Before the conversation died, Tyler looked at the time on his phone and announced he had to get going.

The hardest part was over. Tyler had broken the ice with one group. Now he had a connection with two groups at the school: The Christian circle and Nacho and his buddies.

When Tyler got back to his car, he wrote down everything he could remember. He didn't get Nacho's real name, but he did remember the names of two of the guys in track.

Tyler returned to the campus a week later. Right away he saw Nacho and his buddies sitting at the same table by the snack bar. Nacho was eating nachos again.

"Nacho! Hey—good to see you," Tyler said.

Nacho smiled.

"Hey, Michael—hey, Jake," he said to the two track guys.

They look shocked. As if to say, "He knows my name?"

As Tyler walked over to order some nachos at the snack bar, he overheard another student at the table ask, "Who is that?" One of the other students answered, "He's a priest—I think he is a lunch supervisor." (Students are prone to mix up religious titles.)

When Tyler returned with the nachos, he introduced himself to the new student sitting at the table, "Hey, I'm Tyler."

"What was your favorite movie this summer?" Tyler asked the guys at the table.

That conversation lasted for about five minutes. The students seemed a little more open with him this time. He decided he should try to meet more students and asked for some help. "I'm new here, and I'm totally lost. Can someone give me the tour? I want the inside scoop."

Two of the track guys volunteered, including Michael. They showed Tyler around, which gave him an opportunity to ask more questions about their classes, hobbies, and what they did for fun. Tyler ran track in high school, so he talked distances and times.

They passed a few other students they knew, and Tyler introduced himself. One of the students even asked, "Why are you here?" He told them he was Michael's parole officer, and Michael played along. Tyler cut the tour short and said goodbye so he didn't overextend his welcome.

As he walked away from meeting new students, Tyler tried to commit their names to memory, making a mental note to write the names down when he got to his car.

As Tyler thought about his day, he was happy with the connections he'd made. He had learned a handful of names and some students' interests, and had found some common ground with Michael and another track student named Cameron. His hope was to try to create opportunities to connect with them one-on-one, but he didn't know exactly how to do that.

As the school year continued, Tyler visited the campus at least once a week, sometimes several times a week. One day, Nacho, Michael, Jake, and Cameron were hanging at the table and talking about the early dismissal the next day—they would only have half a day of school because of parent-teacher conferences. Tyler told them he was planning on coming to the school for lunch, but since school was ending early, he offered to treat the four of them to fast food. They seem excited by the offer and agreed.

The next day Tyler waited at a fast-food joint on Main Street, right across the street from the coffee house. The four students showed up, and Tyler treated them to lunch. There were a lot of distractions, as many of the students from the school came in and out, but it was no more distracting than the school cafeteria.

While the other three goofed around, Michael asked Tyler questions about his job. "How long have you been a pastor?" "What made you want to be a pastor?"

It became obvious to Tyler that Michael had something on his mind but was struggling to say it. Michael finally mentioned something about "maybe wanting to go check out church sometime." Tyler said, "It would be great to have you there. Lots of students from the school come to our church. Let me know if you need a ride."

He seemed interested, so Tyler gave him his cell number. Michael entered it into his phone.

Saturday Tyler got a text. "This is Michael. I wanna see if I could go to church with you tomorrow?"

Tyler replied, "Great. Should I stop by today and meet your parents so they know who's taking you?"

There was a long pause.

Finally, Michael responded, "Sure. My mom is here."

When Tyler came to the door, Michael's mom was cordial. She asked him what church he worked at and was quick to mention her church. She tried to explain she'd had trouble getting to church regularly because of work. Later, Michael told Tyler they had really only been to that church twice.

The next morning Tyler picked up Michael for church. Michael seemed to like the service, but Tyler suddenly looked at his new church differently. Throughout the entire morning he worried how Michael would respond. He flinched every time a private joke was mentioned from up front. A few times he leaned over to Michael to explain things as they were announced. For the first time, Tyler realized that most of the people running his church services assumed the entire audience was comprised of mature, growing Christians. They didn't consider someone like Michael would be there.

When they asked people to open up their Bibles, Michael didn't have one. Tyler wondered if he felt dumb for not bringing one, and he quickly flipped to Ephesians and shared his Bible with Michael.

Michael didn't seem to notice these details. He liked the music and appeared to be listening to every word the pastor shared. In addition, he seemed really curious about the midweek youth group announced in the bulletin.

In the car on the way home Tyler asked, "So...what did you think?"

Michael replied, "It seemed pretty cool. I wouldn't mind going again. What is the youth group like?"

Tyler shared about their youth group and dropped Michael off—really encouraged. That Wednesday, Michael saw Tyler on campus and immediately asked if youth group was that night. Tyler responded, "Yeah, it would be great to see you."

After school, Tyler got a text from Michael, "Can Cameron come?"

Within a month Michael brought three of his friends to church and youth group. Michael even brought up the subject at the lunch table at school. The other guys didn't appear to be as curious as Michael. But come Wednesday, several showed up.

On one particular Wednesday, Tyler invited a special speaker to come and give her testimony. She had an amazing story of how God had healed her from abuse and pain in her life. At the end of the service, she gave an invitation. Michael raised his hand, indicating he wanted to put his trust in Christ.

The speaker asked youth workers to meet with the students. So Tyler jumped at the chance to connect with Michael. Michael smiled when he saw him put his hand on his shoulder.

While the worship band played, Tyler asked Michael why he'd raised his hand. He replied, "I want what that speaker had. I want to give my life to God and stuff."

Tyler replied, "That's fantastic. I made the same decision when I was your age. Can I share with you what the Bible says about this?" Michael seemed eager, "Yeah, of course."

Tyler shared about God's love for us and his desire to have a relationship with us. He continued, explaining how sin messes up that relationship because we try to do things our way, not his way. But Jesus breaks down the wall of sin, restoring the path to a relationship with God. Then, Tyler explained we need to truly put our trust in Jesus to restore our relationship with God. "We can't just say, 'Oh, I want to be a Christian,' and then continue trying to do things our way. We need to give up control and put our total trust in Jesus."

Tyler continued, "Jesus will slowly begin to transform us. We won't be perfect, but we'll be a work in progress, slowly becoming more like him. It all starts with a step of faith saying something like, 'God, I'm tired of trying it my way. Forgive me. I want to put my trust in you and let you help me do it your way.'"

Michael prayed right then and there, asking God to forgive him of his past and take control of his future.

Tyler gave him a big hug and talked to him about learning more about his relationship with God. Michael was excited to learn more. So they set up a time to meet before youth group each week and go over a discipleship book.

Many of Michael's friends were still in the not-interested category. Some were willing to check things out and continued to come to church or youth group with Michael.

Tyler continued visiting the campus, meeting new students, learning names, building relationships, and seeking out one-on-one times with students. As he got to know Cameron and Nacho better, he eventually took them each out to the coffee house one-on-one. They weren't as curious as Michael was, but Tyler had some meaningful conversations with each of them and eventually talked with them about God and their beliefs.

Meanwhile, as Tyler was discipling Michael, he had the opportunity to invite his mother to church as well. She began attending with Michael on Sundays, and Michael also got more involved in the youth group.

The process of helping students find Jesus is ongoing. No student is the same. The key is investing in them relationally—*one-on-one.*

CONNECTING WITH DISCIPLESHIP STUDENTS

Outreach			Discipleship		
No Way	Not Interested	Checking Things Out	Stagnant	Growing	Looking for Ministry

The next three chapters are devoted to connecting with *discipleship students.*

All three of these types of *discipleship students* have the same needs: The desire to belong, the need for discipleship, and the longing for an opportunity to use their gifts. In the following chapters we'll talk about how to meet these needs with each of these types of students.

9

ONE-ON-ONE WITH THE STAGNANT KID

Outreach			Discipleship		
No Way	Not Interested	Checking Things Out	Stagnant	Growing	Looking for Ministry

DESCRIPTION:

The *stagnant kids* are the students who made a decision to follow Christ at some time in life but never really grew in faith. They are usually unplugged and can slip in and out of youth group without being noticed. They might attend fun events, but they aren't involved in Bible studies or small groups. They aren't connecting with other students or growing in faith.

OUR GOALS WITH THE *STAGNANT KID:*

Our goals with *stagnant kids* are to build relationships with them and invite them to be discipled, helping transform them into *growing kids*, plugged into church and growing in faith.

Stagnant kids have made a decision to follow Christ at some time in their lives. That should count for something—shouldn't it?

I grew up in the church. Throughout my teenage years, even though I was a trouble-maker, I was highly involved in youth group and student leadership at my church.

In my first two years of college I decided to follow my own path instead of God's path. Then I met Lori (my wife to be). We both decided that our own paths had let to nothing but pain. So we began pursuing God and eventually volunteered as youth leaders together in our church.

After a few years, I took a hiatus from church ministry to work with unchurched students through an on-campus ministry with Youth for Christ.

After a few years of campus ministry, I began volunteering at my church again, while still working on-campus with Youth for Christ. It was at this return to my volunteer work with the church that my eyes were opened. *Many of these church students really weren't much different than the unchurched youth I worked with on campus.*

At the time, the biggest difference I noticed between church students and unchurched students was authenticity. Both students were immersing themselves in the same influences and dabbling in many of the same sins. The church students just tried to hide it.

Unchurched students weren't scared to curse in front of me or talk about lying, cheating, or watching porn. Church students avoided talking about most of these activities until I formed a deep relationship with them and they finally trusted me enough to open up and be honest. But the struggles were the same with both groups of students.

In the last decade I've noticed church students becoming much more real about who they are. Teenagers are sharing their inner-most thoughts on a public forum—places like MySpace and Facebook. In many ways, students are more transparent today about who they really are.

The distinction between churched and unchurched students is rapidly shrinking. When we look at day-to-day decisions, most churched students act just like unchurched students. They listen to the same music, browse the same Web sites, and watch the same television and movies. Churched and unchurched students lie, cheat, and gossip just the same. For example, just a few years ago Barna did a study about music piracy. Active church attenders (78 percent) were just as likely as nonattenders (81 percent) to engage in piracy.[xxiii] When it all comes down to the little daily moral decisions like burning a CD for a friend, lying to mom or dad, or cheating on an exam—our church students really aren't that different from their unchurched counterparts.

The more we grow to understand and interact with *outreach students*, the better equipped we'll be to help our *discipleship students*. This is especially true with our *stagnant kids.* These students aren't growing, and they aren't plugged into God's people. They are being influenced more by the three "I"s than anything else: *Internet, iPods* and *ignorance. Stagnant kids* are more apt to look at the newest MTV drama for relationship advice than they would from the church.

So how do we reach them? How can we plug them in? It all starts with an investment of time.

TIME

It happens all the time. One overworked youth worker, a handful of volunteers, and not enough time in the day. Students float in and out of youth group, Sunday worship, and a myriad of activities. We don't want any students to slip through the cracks, but we only have so much time and so many volunteers.

So which students get the investment of time? Often, time goes to those who show up.

Think about it. Those *fringe students*, as we call them, are hard to connect with. We try to go up and talk with them in the back row on Sunday morning, but they don't seem interested. We invite them to summer camp and our fall retreat, but they never come.

We think to ourselves, "It's her choice. I'm not going to force her into anything. I've given them multiple chances to be involved."

Have you really? Have you ever asked if you could go to lunch?

My friend Matt is a junior high pastor at a large church. He often has 200 to 300 junior high students on Wednesday nights and Sunday mornings. Imagine trying to invest time into all of those students.

His Wednesday-night program was focused on worship. Even though they attended each week, Jake, Brock, and Andrew didn't take worship seriously.

These three boys were easily the most popular students in the group. They were good looking, and each enjoyed the title of "big man on campus" at school. The problem was, everyone had their eyes on these three. If Jake, Brock, and Andrew weren't worshiping, 50 other students weren't worshiping. If those three started goofing around and doing crazy dance moves during a song, the whole room would soon follow.

Whenever Matt or any of the youth leaders was teaching, these three tuned out. They were far more interested in the girls who surrounded them than anything spiritual.

After correcting them countless times, Matt was ready to ask them to quit coming on Wednesdays.

After praying about it, he felt he should connect with them and talk with them face-to-face before making any decisions. All his interaction with them had been at youth group, and the longest conversation he'd had with any of them was probably two minutes. Matt realized maybe he needed to invest in them a little more before he made any drastic decisions.

So Matt and one of his interns took the three boys out for dinner. Matt really enjoyed their time together. Jake was the rowdy one in the bunch, but Brock was the leader of the three. Andrew seemed to be just along for the food. They laughed as they ate and talked together. This was the first real conversation Matt had ever had with any of the boys.

After dinner Matt and his intern brought the three boys to their school campus. The sun was setting, and the campus was empty.

Matt grabbed a picnic table in the open grassy area in the center of the school (California schools often have a central outdoor area where students hang out en masse). Sitting in the middle of the campus, Matt began to talk with the boys.

"Do you know you are leaders?"

The boys looked at each other and didn't answer.

"You do realize how popular you are, don't you?"

Jake broke the silence, "Yeah, I guess so." Brock and Andrew agreed.

Matt continued, "You three are being watched at school, after school, and at youth group. If one of you chooses to act a certain way, then others follow."

The boys were listening to every word. Matt looked at each one of them and continued, "Do you realize this?"

"I guess," Brock responded, as if to say, *So? What are you getting at?*

Matt got to the point, "People follow you. That makes you leaders. And with leadership comes great responsibility. The question I want you to think about is, *Where are you leading everyone?*"

Matt pulled out his Bible and flipped through the pages until he found John 10:10. He looked up at the boys and said, "Jesus said something I want you to hear." Matt read slowly, looking up from his Bible to connect eyes with each of the boys at several intervals during his reading of the verse.

"The thief comes only to steal and kill and destroy; I have come that they may have life, and have it to the full."

Matt closed the Bible, keeping the page with his thumb. "Jesus talks about two forces at work here: Those that are here to destroy and those that give life." He paused for a moment, and then he asked them a question, "Which one are you?"

Matt explained they had a choice to make. They could either lead people toward destruction, or they could lead people toward that which is good, Jesus being the perfect example of this—the giver of life to the fullest. Again he asked them, "Which one do you want to be?"

The boys hung their heads low. They knew the direction they had been leading people, and it wasn't good. The choice was clear, but it wasn't easy.

It was Jake who spoke first again, this time with less confidence. "I don't want to lead people toward anything bad." He looked at his friends, wondering if he was alone in this endeavor.

Silence.

He returned his gaze to Matt, "I want to be a leader for good." He looked over at Brock and Andrew again.

Brock seemed to be lost in thought, his brow wrinkled, his gaze downward. Andrew was a mystery. No one knew what he was thinking.

Brock broke the silence, "I'm in."

Andrew chimed in a second later, "Me too."

The five of them held hands in the middle of the campus and prayed. By the time the prayer was done, not one of them was without tears in his eyes.

As Matt took the students home, he asked if they wanted to meet again. They all agreed. Matt, his intern, and the boys exchanged cell phone numbers, and Matt told them to text him if they needed him.

Matt thought about the whole situation on the drive home. He had contemplated kicking the three of them out of the group. Instead, he'd met with them face-to-face. His connection with them launched the journey of three *stagnant kids* committing themselves to becoming *growing kids*.

It's amazing what an investment of time can accomplish in the lives of students.

RELATIONSHIPS FIRST

Stagnant kids in many ways are most like *not-interested kids*. In the church we have labels for this group, nicknames like *fringe students* or even *complacent Christians*. I almost find it easier to interact with *checking-things-out kids* because at least they *realize* they're missing something. *Stagnant kids* figure they're okay because they attend church. Consequently, it's not always easy to impact this group through our programming.

Youth workers regularly ask me, "What do I do with the students I have who are uncommitted and unplugged?" In other words, "What do I do with my *stagnant kids*?"

My response is almost always the same, "Are you and your leaders meeting with these students one-on-one?"

Typically, the answer is no. Helping a *stagnant kid* grow spiritually usually begins with a relationship. I find it easy to break the ice with these kids. They might be resistant to our programming, but they aren't resistant to social interaction. *Stagnant kids*, by definition, have already accepted Christ. Often they have grown up in the church or at least attended some sort of church activities. This makes it easier for a youth worker to contact them and take them out for ice cream or coffee. Connecting with them can be as easy as a phone call: "Hey, Brian. I haven't seen you in a while. Let me take you out for a soda after school sometime this week."

For many of us, it is easy to overlook these students—just like my friend Matt who realized, "I've never really had a conversation with these guys for more than two minutes."

Seek out opportunities to connect with them. Try to get with them one-on-one.

If you find it difficult to connect with a *stagnant kid*—no worries. Just back up a few steps, apply what you read in the previous chapters, and use some of the recommendations for breaking the ice with a *not-interested kid* or a *no-way kid*.

SIDE NOTE: That's what's amazing about working with *outreach students*. If you can talk with a *no-way kid*, you can talk with anyone. I'd recommend all youth workers, especially those who want to make a career out of youth ministry, work for an outreach organization (Young Life, Youth for Christ, Fellowship of Christian Athletes, etc...) for at least one year. This experience of connecting with *outreach students* is priceless.

In a previous chapter I talked about using basketball to break the ice with guys. Female youth workers will attest to the fact that sleepovers are excellent opportunities for relationship building. Have five girls over for a girls' night. Once all toenails have been painted, facial masks have been washed off, and the giggling has subsided, the girls will usually have some very deep conversations with you—and each other. One youth worker told me if she had just two to three girls to sleep over at a time, it was the most effective. They love the attention and will really open up in such an intimate setting.

DEEPER CONVERSATIONS

Once we have a relationship with a student, we can begin to talk about deeper issues. Our fun conversations about basketball stars and favorite TV shows can transition to sharing feelings, emotions, and struggles. Those issues usually bring up questions about how to cope. Real issues are an open door to deeper conversations.

Here's a sample of how a fun conversation with a *stagnant kid* might lead to talking about deeper issues. (I've also included notes about the direction of the conversation.)

Youth worker: "I'm glad you get to hang out with me after school like this. What do you usually do after school?"

Student: "Not much. I just do my homework… maybe watch a little TV."

Youth worker: "Oh, yeah? What shows do you like?"

Student: "I dunno—just whatever." (This is a common answer from teenagers. "I dunno." So we need to be ready to ask the question another way or try something else. Multiple choice may be a good option.)

Youth worker: "Do you watch any reality TV like *American Idol* or any of the Real World shows like *Laguna Beach?*" (Here I threw out two TV choices that are reality shows. One is clean: *American Idol*. The other is an MTV show, pure garbage. This can tell me a lot about what the student is filling his head with.)

Student: "I watch a little *American Idol* and sometimes *So You Think You Can Dance.*" (The student bypassed my MTV reference completely.)

Youth worker: "What's your favorite show?"

Student: "Probably *Family Guy.*"

Youth worker: "Ha! What do you like about it?"

Student: "It's funny."

Youth worker: "So what's your favorite thing to do for fun during a typical week." (I added "during a typical week" to keep the answers based in reality, as opposed to, "Go to Disneyland!")

Student: "I dunno. Probably just hang with my friends."

Youth worker: "Where do you hang?"

Student: "Wherever. Rian's house." (Aha…here's an open door.)

Youth worker: "Anything particularly fun about Rian's house?"

Student: "Not really—his mom's pretty cool."

Youth worker: "I had a friend with a mom like that. How's she cool?"

Student: "She always feeds us, and she doesn't get on our case for stupid stuff."

Youth worker: "Nice, who does get on your case for stupid stuff?"

Student: "My mom."

Youth worker: "What about your stepdad? Is that who I met when I picked you up"? (In chapter 13 you'll hear more from me about the importance of meeting the parents before spending one-on-one time with students.)

Student: "Dave? He's worse. He just tells us to get out of the room because he's tired from work."

Youth worker: "So Rian's house feels a little safer?"

Student: "Yeah, I guess. Just more fun, that's all."

Youth worker: "So who do you go to if you want to talk about something?" (Boom—I turned the corner to a deeper question.)

Student: "I dunno—no one really. Maybe my mom... if Dave's not around. She's different when he's around."

Youth worker: "It's important to have someone to talk to."

Student: "I guess."

Youth worker: "I'll tell you what. If you ever need someone to listen, I'll make time."

Student: "Thanks."

Youth worker: 'What's your cell number?"

Student: "Uh... 555-2948."

Youth worker: "I'm calling you right now. Do ya see the incoming call?"

Student: "Yeah."

Youth worker: "Cool, save me in your contacts. Text or call me any time if you need to talk about something."

Student: "Okay."

Youth worker: "Hey—all this ice cream is giving me brain freeze. Let's go across the street and check out that sport store. I have to buy a pair of running shoes." (I changed the subject quickly since this was our first meeting.)

Some of you might wonder why I didn't bust out my King James Bible right there and start preaching about the importance of fellowship. Our goal is to plug him in, right? Yes, but at the same time we don't want to scare him away.

In the above conversation I moved from, *"What do you usually do after school?"* to, *"So who do you go to if you want to talk about something?"* His answer revealed she doesn't really have someone to talk to outside of his mom. I used that as an opportunity to let him know I was there for him if he needed a listening ear. Then I let him off the hook by changing the subject quickly.

I've said it before in this book: Face-to-face conversation can be very difficult for teenagers today. Therefore I don't want my one-on-one conversations to seem awkward or too invasive in any way.

After multiple meetings these conversations will become more comfortable. Think of friendships you have now. At first, the conversations were probably a little awkward. But as you got to know each other, you each relaxed and let down your walls.

As you build a relationship, you will find greater opportunities to talk about deeper issues.

I find it easy to transition to conversations about Christ when I'm talking with *stagnant kids*. They've been exposed to the gospel already, and many of them have attended church quite a bit. They've had spiritual conversations, they just haven't given Christ control of their lives.

Wait a minute. They haven't given Christ control? Are they even Christians?

DON'T ASSUME THEY'RE BELIEVERS

Here's where the categories in our table get a little less clear. By definition, *stagnant kids* are believers. They accepted Christ as some point in life, but some would argue *stagnant kids* aren't actual believers because they haven't given God control. Others might argue they once believed but have now lost salvation.

Is it worth debating? How's this: I just don't want them to be stagnant any more.

Let's put our energy into the future.

Often, I find *stagnant kids* need to hear the gospel again, whether it's so they can accept Christ for real or just recommit. We need to provide opportunities for these students to give Christ control of their lives.

In my years working with church students, I've shared Christ with many *stagnant kids*. After sharing the gospel with them, I've actually had some of them say, "I've never heard it like that."

I promise you, I just share the gospel truth: *God's love for us, our sin, Jesus paying for that sin, and our need to put faith in him.* I usually share a story and some Scripture and end by asking, "Where do you stand?" Just like Matt did with the three boys at the picnic table in the middle of the campus, "Which one of these do you want to be?"

Don't assume *stagnant kids* are already believers. Many of them still need to surrender to Christ, some of them need the gospel explained clearly, and some need you to ask them the tough questions. But our time with *stagnant kids* doesn't end with sharing the gospel.

DISCIPLESHIP

As you continue meeting with these students, look for an opportunity to invite them to become more involved in church and discipleship.

Our process with *stagnant kids* might look like this:

- Create opportunities to connect *one-on-one*

- Open the door to deeper conversations

- Share the gospel

- Ask to meet regularly to study the Bible or go through a discipleship book

Discipleship is the key to helping a *stagnant kid* grow. By discipleship, I simply mean an adult mentor meeting with a student one-on-one for biblical study, prayer, and a time of encouragement. Most often the reason students are stagnant is because no one has invested in them and discipled them. Discipleship makes all the difference.

We need to initiate discipleship by connecting adult mentors with our *discipleship students*. All three *discipleship students* (*stagnant kids, growing kids,* and *looking-for-ministry kids*) need to be discipled. In particular, *stagnant kids* desperately need it.

Whenever I build relationships with *stagnant kids*, I find it pretty easy to transition to a discipleship relationship. Usually I've already initiated contact with the student by taking him out for french fries or ice cream. It is then natural to ask, "Hey, this is fun. Would you like to keep meeting like this?"

I've never had a student say no.

The first thing I do is suggest how we could spend our time together. My first choice is always to go through a discipleship book of some kind. We have a free book to download on our Web site called *Welcome to the Family*. I've asked numerous students if they would like to meet weekly and go through that book. With other students, I may suggest a book more appropriate to a current struggle. Other times I suggest a book of the Bible such as Ephesians. I also make sure we keep the time fun. I don't want the student to think, *Now that we're going through this book, we don't have fun anymore. Being a Christian is boring.*

Make sure you keep hanging out for fun. Keep asking questions about life—keep listening. Make the study time a priority, but don't lose the relational time.

PLUGGING IN

Remember, our goal with *stagnant kids* is to see them growing and plugged into a church family. *Stagnant kids* don't commonly plug into groups because they don't feel like they belong: "I don't know anyone. I don't relate to those people."

Your mentor relationships with students can make those feelings disappear. Helping *stagnant kids* get plugged in takes time. Invite them to safe, fun times with just a few students, bring them to group activities, and slowly introduce them to other students. Provide safe venues such as small groups where they can easily connect. These basics will help *stagnant kids* begin to plug in.

GRADUATING FROM STAGNATION

As you invest time with *stagnant kids*, they'll begin to grow, and they'll become more active in your youth group and congregation. One-on-one attention can totally change the attitudes of the students we work with.

My friend Karl witnessed this. Karl has a thriving ministry, but as with any ministry, a small population of *stagnant kids* floated in and out. One of these stagnates was a student named Vincent. Vincent was rich and spoiled and only went to church when he felt like it. Karl tried to connect with Vincent his freshman year, but Vincent was not interested. He attended fun activities but never showed up for anything deep. The beginning of Vincent's sophomore year, Karl made a major shift in the programming of his youth ministry. He canceled one of the fun nights and started a weekly service project where students would serve other people in the church. When Vincent heard the fun night was canceled, he threw a fit. His mom even called Karl to tell him Vincent probably wouldn't be attending anymore. Karl said, "Just let me talk with him sometime this week."

Karl called Vincent and asked him for his help. He said, "Vincent, I've gotta be honest with you. Last year your attitude stunk. Do you agree?"

There was a silence on the other end of the phone. He wondered if he'd come on too strong, but a second later he finally heard, "Yeah...I guess."

Karl continued, "I'm not worried about it. It was your freshman year. Freshmen have enough pressures to worry about. I know my freshman year was one of the most difficult in my life." Karl continued, "But now you're a sophomore. I expect more from you, and honestly, I need your help."

Karl says there was a new energy on the other end of the line. "Sure, what do you need?"

Karl explained he really needed some of the students who had been there to help with the transition. He brainstormed some of the ideas with Vincent and asked for his input. When Vincent made a suggestion, Karl asked if Vincent could help him make it happen. Vincent enthusiastically agreed. Karl concluded by asking Vincent to help him by encouraging others to be a part of these new opportunities to serve.

Later that night Karl received a phone call. It was Vincent's mother. "I don't know what you said to Vincent, but he's a different student. He's all excited about the service project next week, and he's been texting his friends about it all day." She repeatedly thanked Karl.

Vincent is now plugged into the ministry and is a key part of the weekly service projects. He's not perfect, but he's growing more and is involved. Vincent is also part of a small group now, and his small group leader meets with him one-on-one.

Vincent moved from being a *stagnant kid* to a *growing kid*— and it all started with a simple phone call asking for his help and involvement.

10
ONE-ON-ONE WITH THE *GROWING KID*

Outreach			Discipleship		
No Way	Not Interested	Checking Things Out	Stagnant	Growing	Looking for Ministry

DESCRIPTION:

Growing kids are exactly who we want our *outreach* and *stagnant kids* to become: Plugged into God's people (the church), and growing in their relationships with Jesus. *Growing kids* have put their trust in Jesus and are allowing him to transform their lives slowly.

OUR GOALS WITH THE *GROWING KID:*

Our goals with *growing kids* are to build relationships with them, disciple them, and equip them to live out their faith day to day. We also need to help them begin to discover their spiritual gifts, giving them opportunities to serve others.

Joshua seemed to be a *growing kid* forever. He was plugged into the high school youth group and excited about his faith. But the one thing Joshua seemed to lack was...*growth* (rather paradoxical for a *growing kid*).

Joshua was involved in a small group, he worshiped, and he was engaged with the teaching. Joshua showed all the signs of a *growing kid*. He just wasn't moving to the right in the *six-types-of-students* table.

Maybe that was because Joshua was never given an opportunity to serve in ministry or use his gifts.

One day the sound guy didn't show up on a Sunday morning (unfortunately, a pretty regular occurrence). Stephen, the youth pastor, saw Josh sitting quietly by himself and grabbed him. "Josh. I need a favor. Can you come back here and run sound?" Stephen gave Josh a brief lesson on how to run the sound board, and Josh seemed happy to help.

As the service ended, Stephen thanked Josh profusely. Stephen noticed Josh really responded well to the opportunity to help. So he asked Josh, "Would you like to help again next week?" Josh welcomed the invitation to serve.

The next Sunday Joshua was waiting by the door when Stephen arrived. "I burned some CDs this week that I thought would be good to play on a Sunday morning." Stephen smiled, "Joshua—my man!"

Week after week Joshua became more involved. When sign-ups for the student-leadership team happened, Stephen asked Joshua to apply. "We need you on this team Joshua."

Soon Joshua became a very active part of the student-leadership team. When he graduated from high school, Joshua became one of Stephen's volunteers and helped with the junior high ministry. Now he has a full-time position with the church as a youth ministry resident.

In a recent staff meeting someone asked Joshua, "What was one of the most significant experiences in your spiritual journey?"

Joshua didn't even blink, "When I was asked to serve."

Joshua sat in that youth ministry for two years doing everything he was asked to do. He had heard numerous announcements about student leadership but wasn't sure how he could contribute. But when Joshua was asked to serve one week, it changed his life.

Growing kids won't continue to grow if they aren't challenged to serve and use their gifts.

Who are our *growing kids*?

THESE ARE OUR "GOOD" STUDENTS

Growing kids are not perfect, but they have given God control. They want to do what's right. They are Acts 2:42 in action: Devoted to the apostles' teaching (studying the truth of Scripture), prayer (worship and times of solitude with God), the breaking of bread (the Lord's Supper), and fellowship (hanging out with other Christians).

After dealing with the previous four types of students, the *growing kid* is a snap. Think about it. This student is plugged in, connected, and growing in faith. Toss this student a Bible and let 'em be. Right? Okay—maybe I'm getting a little carried away.

Remember what I said in the last chapter: The moral divide between church students and unchurched students is rapidly shrinking. Many churched students are immersing themselves in the same pool of influences as those outside of church, causing them to become quite similar in action and belief.

A couple years ago I was asked to speak at a camp in the South. The leaders of the camp informed me, "This week might be a little different than most weeks for you. These are our good students."

The camp was full of church students who came to the camp specifically to learn more about the Bible and grow in faith—textbook *growing kids*. One of the subjects the leaders wanted me to cover was the subject of "God's plan for sex." I was happy to talk about it, but I needed some clarification. "Do you want me just to touch on the subject, or really hit them with what they need to hear?" I asked honestly.

"I want you to tell them the truth," he quickly replied.

"The truth about the choices these students are making isn't exactly rated G," I pointed out.

This seemed to make this particular leader a little uncomfortable. "Remember," he clarified, "these are our good students."

I proposed an idea. I told him I'd take a little survey of sorts from the stage, and based on what I heard from the audience, I'd adjust my content. He agreed. Two hours later I stood on stage in front of about 200 students and asked them a candid question, "Do you want to know the truth?"

With Bibles open they stared at me for a moment, perplexed. Slowly, I began to see nods and hear the word *yes* being said around the room. "Okay, but I need to know the truth from you first. So I have to ask you, can you be honest with me?"

Again, heads began nodding and students said yes. This was my fourth day speaking to this group, morning and night. I'd spent the week with them, had eaten every meal with them, and knew many of them by name. They were getting pretty comfortable with me.

I asked them all to bow their heads and close their eyes. Then I asked the adult leaders to do the same. I told the adult leaders, "These students have committed to be honest with us. So, no peeking—agreed?" All the adult leaders said yes.

I explained to the students, with their heads down and eyes closed, I was going to name some media influences: Movies, music, and the Internet. And if they had looked at any of these influences, with everyone's eyes closed (I reminded them again), I wanted them to stand up and remain standing.

I said, "If you've seen any of these movies in the theater, on DVD, or on cable (*not* the edited TV versions, the normal, R-rated versions) please stand up." Then I began listing movies. *Hostile*, any of the *American Pie* films, *Wedding Crashers*, etc..." Every film I named was full of nudity and over-the-top, crude, sexual content. By the fifth title, almost 80 percent of the room was standing up.

I went on with my list, "If you've ever looked at porn intentionally more than once, please stand up." Even more stood. "If you have any albums with explicit lyrics from artists like 50 Cent, Li'l Wayne, or Justin Timberlake..." I went on. I named artists whose content I knew was overtly sexual—lyrics you don't even want to hear once. These are lyrics students in this generation of young people subject themselves to for hours each day.

More and more students stood.

Finally, I ended with TV. I named TV shows that were over the top with sexual content like Tila Tequila and *Gossip Girl*.

When I finished my list, only four students remained sitting.

Let me be clear: I'm not saying if a student watches *Gossip Girl* once, she is now not "good." My point is this: Most of our students are regularly subjecting themselves to false messages and drowning themselves in sexual content. But when we speak to them about issues like sex, we are afraid to be direct, afraid to offend.

We need to speak truth. More importantly, we need to be aware of what our students are being besieged with daily. Many of our *discipleship students* are surrounding themselves with the same temptations and listening to the same modern-day philosophers our *outreach students* are. Yes, we want to give these students an opportunity to serve, but service opportunities for these students shouldn't be handed out without discipleship and accountability. We need to build our students up on foundations of faith. They need to learn and meditate on the Scriptures so they can be strong when they face temptation and so they can be equipped to answer tough questions.

Many of the students I meet in churches today have very little knowledge or understanding of the Scriptures. Most of them reflect the attitudes and beliefs of pop culture rather than biblical truth.

Recently, my wife Lori volunteered at our church to lead my daughter's junior high small group. Small groups were clearly designed for *growing kids* who were committed to Jesus—"good church students."

Around Easter, the small group discussion turned toward Jesus' claims of being the only way. One girl in Lori's group raised her hand and asked with a perplexed look on her face, "But is that saying if someone doesn't believe in Jesus, they're going to hell?"

Before Lori had a chance to answer, another girl in the group spoke up, "Yeah, my cousin's Jewish. What about her? She believes in God."

Another girl interjected, "I don't think God would send anyone to hell. What if there was a person on a desert island who didn't even know. That would be cruel."

Lori didn't have a chance to respond. The girl with the Jewish cousin jumped right in again, "I think all religions probably believe the same thing, and their people are okay as long as they really mean it."

Lori tried to answer the questions and talk with the girls, but it soon became obvious all these girls had been saturated in other messages from our culture. Lori came home with her stomach in knots. "It was so hard to answer these questions, and when I did, I don't think they wanted to hear it."

Lori had worked with unchurched students for a decade. I'd never before seen her that frazzled. These were supposed to be our committed church students.

Therefore, don't assume our *growing kids* know the Bible and daily apply it to their thoughts and actions. The fact is, most of them are probably spending a lot more time being influenced by the voices in our culture than they are listening to truth. When many of them leave high school, that will be the end of church participation.

But we can reverse that pattern with one-on-one discipleship.

KNOWING THE *GROWING KID*

As I began studying how media and pop culture affect our church kids, I realized many of them are not being prepared for life after high school.

Are your kids ready to face the questions, temptations, and modern philosophies that will bombard them when they leave home and your youth group? When they are removed from the safety of their current surroundings and shipped off like Daniel to Babylon, will your kids "resolve not to defile themselves"?

Many of our kids just aren't "getting it," slipping in and out of church each week. They don't own their own faith. I've seen youth workers respond to this problem in numerous ways. The most popular seems to be teaching apologetics.

I'm all for apologetics. I just don't think we can rely on up-front teaching alone. Teaching an entire group is definitely an efficient way to get information out to large numbers, but this venue doesn't allow us to answer the questions people are afraid to ask when part of a group. It also doesn't give us the opportunity to help navigate difficult conversations and situations.

What's the best way to do this? Through one-on-one discipleship.

ONE-ON-ONE DISCIPLESHIP NEEDED

Our *growing kids* are in desperate need of being grounded in faith—they need *discipleship*. A youth worker named Josh describes how one-on-one discipleship helped a *growing kid* get a vision for ministry:

> I had a neighbor named Anton who I got to know pretty well. After building a relationship with him, I invited him to camp. At the end of camp, Anton accepted Christ. He was on fire, so I thought I should ask him if he wanted me to disciple him. I asked him if he'd be interested in getting to know God deeper, and he was excited by this opportunity.
>
> We began to meet once a week for about an hour. We started at square one, talking about prayer, faith, who Jesus was, assurance of salvation, etc…
>
> Since he was a neighbor, he saw me a lot. Whenever he saw my car in the driveway, he'd come over, and we would hang out.
>
> The next year he came to camp with us again. After camp Anton said he felt a call into ministry (which we could all see). Now he has been interning here all summer. He is a big help at the church and in our youth ministry. I can't wait for some more opportunities to employ his gifts and talents.

One-on-one discipleship time can be used as a time of encouragement and development. It might start with the basics, as in the case of Josh and Anton above. Hopefully, it will progress to something much deeper. You can begin to help your *growing kids* discover their gifts by giving them opportunities to use them.

Recently a youth worker named PJ told me a story about a student in his group named Calvin.

> I'll never forget how coffee changed our youth ministry forever.
>
> When Calvin first came to our student ministry, he did everything he could to fit in. He was loud, obnoxious, and kind of annoying. He tried too hard to be who he thought everyone wanted him to be.
>
> During one typical midweek service, I shared about a former student I'd had named Alex, a student who had a lot of potential but decided to live life his own way and walk away from God. It was a story with a sad ending. Calvin approached me after and asked to talk. He told me the story had touched him. Then he said, "PJ, I don't wanna be an Alex. I want my life to count."
>
> He asked if we could meet weekly, and if I'd mentor him. Our coffee journey began. At first it was mostly small talk, and every now and then we would hit a tender subject. During one of our visits, sitting there drinking "devil's brew" (coffee), I confronted Calvin with some stuff in his life. It was amazing; he loved me for pushing him and thanked me for being honest. Calvin began to grow in leadership. I began to give him responsibilities in our youth services, and boy, did he shine. Weeks passed and he kept growing.

At one of our regular weekly meetings we were discussing *Heroes*, the popular TV show. We were joking and making fun of the characters, and all of the sudden it turned into a brainstorming session. Man, the ideas were flowing, and we were on a roll. By the time we ended, we had created an entire four-week message series for our student ministry. The series exploded with funny video clips, quirky *Heroes* characterizations, and awesome memories. I was so blown away I decide to use the theme for an upcoming retreat. Calvin even helped me write the script for the main sessions.

It all started because one unique student named Calvin was given the opportunity to hang with his youth pastor at a coffee shop and learn to use his talents for the glory of God.

PJ was able to help Alex develop his gifts and abilities. It didn't take long for PJ to discover Alex had a knack for creative writing. PJ helped Alex bring some of his ideas to fruition.

But PJ also had the opportunity to talk to Alex about things Alex wouldn't have shared in a group. PJ was able to push and encourage him in areas that required one-on-one attention. Sometimes our *growing kids* need a little push. This is called accountability.

ACCOUNTABILITY

Accountability doesn't mean changing our role from encourager to parole officer. This means continuing our role of encouragement, mixed with a good balance of tough questions.

A few months ago I sat by the pool with a young man from our church. He was listening to his iPod, so I used that as a means to start the conversation.

"What are you listening to?"

He hesitated and then said, "Oh nothing much."

I knew this student pretty well, so I pressed a little deeper. "What?" I teased him, "Are you scared to tell me what you're listening to?"

He smiled, "No." He didn't want to seem like he had anything to hide, so he told me the song name. It wasn't a bad song, but it was a secular song—maybe that explained his initial hesitation.

I told him honestly, "Oh, I like that song. Can I hear it?"

He handed me his iPod. He seemed happy to let me hear it, possibly because few adults had ever taken an interest in what he listened to.

 When the song was done, I asked, "I'm always curious about the kinds of music people like. Do you mind if I look at some of your music on here?" He agreed, with some concern on his face.

(NOTE: Never flip through a student's iPod or phone without asking permission.)

I immediately spun my thumbs over to the most-recently-played list. You can always learn something about a student from that list. I saw a bunch of raunchy songs on the list, so I started asking him about them—not accusingly—just in a curious way. "Wow, did you buy this one?"

"No," he said, a little embarrassed. "I got that from my friend."

I looked at him for a second with a confused look on my face. He proceeded to explain to me how to hook up an iPod to a friend's computer and download free songs off iTunes manually.

I was only three minutes into this conversation, and I was already learning volumes of information about the kind of music this young man listened to and his stance on downloading music illegally.

We began talking about music, what he liked and what he didn't like. We talked about lyrics and possible effects. The conversation opened up numerous doors for future conversations.

Walking away from the situation, I was amazed at what I'd learned about this young man from his iPod. I was also able to use what I'd learned to talk with him about issues in his Christian faith.

As mentors, we can use moments like these as teaching moments.

My friend Wendy, a youth worker in Iowa, sent me this story about Stacey.

> Stacey accepted Christ at the age of 12 but had never received any follow-up. She began sporadically attending our youth group when she was in junior high. Following her freshman year in high school, Stacey started to get more involved. She joined a Bible study, the youth choir, and our student-leadership team. She also began regularly coming on Sunday mornings to our Student Bible Fellowship and church.
>
> During her junior and senior years, she started to serve, helping with children's church and new Christian follow-up and coleading a junior high girls' Bible study with a peer. Throughout this time, I had the opportunity to mentor her.

Our mentoring relationship began when I found her crying after youth group one night. Our topic that evening had hit her pretty hard, and she began to confide in me regarding some very sensitive emotional issues in her life. A week later we met at my house and had a deep conversation about these issues. What followed was two years of mentoring and friendship.

We spent time together weekly, sometimes daily, just talking about life stuff and praying together. The fruit of this mentoring relationship cultivated one evening when Stacey had to make a difficult phone call, and she wanted me sitting beside her for support and assistance. She made the call to a male friend who was having a difficult time making wise choices in his relationship with his girlfriend. What transpired was a mentor's bittersweet dream: She didn't need me. I did not even need to be next to her because she handled it beautifully—tough love honesty seasoned with Scripture and encouragement. I am thankful God chose to use me in his work of shaping Stacey.

When I told Wendy I was going to use her story in the book, she emailed Stacey. Stacey replied with this note to Wendy.

Wendy,

I am surprised my life is a story worth sharing. But reading it in print and looking back, I thank God you were there. I don't know if some of this drama would be over today if it wasn't for you taking time to shake me into reality and helping me get over the original issues I faced when you started mentoring me. You are always going to be one of the most important people who made me exactly who I am today!

– Stacey

I can't even begin to count how many times I've heard a young believer say almost the exact same words: *If it wasn't for "Wendy," I wouldn't be who I am today.*

TECHNOLOGY

Technology has become a great tool to help build accountability. When appropriate, text messaging can be a great way to keep accountable with our students. Students can text us when they face a temptation; and we can text them at specific times to encourage them when they ask us for prayer.

Social networking sites can also be a great place to provide encouragement and accountability. Numerous Christian sites have emerged that can provide a safe place to connect. Your entire small group of girls or guys could form a network and post songs, links, or notes of encouragement for all to see. Of course, adults contacting teens through technology also brings up some necessary concerns. We'll talk about those in chapter 13.

VITAL CARE

The message of this chapter is simple:

- Connect *growing kids* with caring adults who will give them one-on-one attention

- Disciple students one-on-one

- Provide accountability

- Give students an opportunity to serve

I try not to speak in absolutes very often when I write. I don't want to be the guy who says, "Do this and you'll be successful." Usually I prefer to say, "Hey, this helped me, maybe it will help you, too." But I'm going to step out of that box for a moment and say something as absolutely as I can. I believe this with my whole heart: *If we aren't connecting our students with adult mentors, we are making a huge mistake.*

Let me put it another way. If you can think of a student who's coming to your group week in and week out—but he doesn't have an adult who contacts him and takes him out for french fries— then you need to make some changes in your ministry.

I know that might seem difficult for larger ministries. If you have 300 students weekly, you might wonder if one-on-one mentoring is even possible. But the great thing is most groups of 300 come from larger churches that have a greater numbers of adults who can mentor.

If your group has 12 students, make it your goal to have at least three adults who can keep in contact with four students each. Groups of 300 should strive to have 60 adults working with students, allowing each adult to connect with five students. (We'll talk more about how to make this happen in chapter 14).

Intentionally caring for students is vital to the health of our students. One-on-one attention can make all the difference.

11

ONE-ON-ONE WITH THE LOOKING-FOR-MINISTRY KID

Outreach			Discipleship		
No Way	Not Interested	Checking Things Out	Stagnant	Growing	Looking for Ministry

DESCRIPTION:

Looking-for-ministry kids are not only growing in their faith daily, they are looking for opportunities to minister in everyday situations. These students are our leaders and the future of the church.

OUR GOALS WITH THE *LOOKING-FOR-MINISTRY KID:*

Our goals with *looking-for-ministry kids* are to build relationships with them, continue discipling them, and train and develop them for leadership and service.

Call me crazy, but my favorite kinds of students are the *no-way kids* and the *looking-for-ministry kids.* I love 'em both. They both are committed to what they choose to believe. So what makes the *looking-for-ministry kids* different from other students?

They want to reach out to their friends.

Years ago my friend Kurt Johnston and I had a conversation about effective outreach—it's a conversation I'll never forget. As the junior high director at Saddleback, he runs some pretty large programs. I asked him what his most effective outreach tool was. His answer was, "My students."

Kurt is a huge advocate of friendship evangelism. The concept is simple. Students who want to make a difference in the lives of their friends commit to a three-step strategy:

1. Live an authentic Christian life.

2. Pray for opportunities to share your faith.

3. Communicate with love.

Kurt explained why he invests so much energy and attention on this approach to evangelism:

> The reason I believe so strongly in Friendship Evangelism—as flawed as it is—is because I believe big on-going outreach programs handicap our students in the long run. I don't want them to rely on me, the church, our budget, our facilities, etc…to reach their friends. I want them to see early on that a program doesn't change a life, but a relationship does. If a student leaves Saddleback and goes to a tiny little church in the Midwest with two students and no outreach program, I want that student to have the understanding that she is the outreach

program. It may not click right now while they're in a big, happening environment, but I'm hoping that we're planting seeds of maturity in their hearts that will reap results when it matters most.

If you don't know Kurt, you might assume a church like Saddleback has flashy programs to reach students. But flashy takes second chair to students reaching students in Kurt's ministry. The simple concept of *looking-for-ministry kids* reaching out to their friends trumps laser lighting and smoke machines any day.

Students reaching students sounds great, but how can we get our students to do this? In other words, how do we prepare our *looking-for-ministry kids* to actually *look for ministry*?

MOVING TO THE ... *LEFT?*

Up until this point in the book our goal has been to move students to the right on our *six-types-of-students* table. Our *looking-for-ministry kids* are already to the far right. So what should we do with them? Leave them there?

We need to equip them to move to the left.

Huh?

Our *looking-for-ministry kids* bring new life to our *six-types-of-students* table. They are the influencers who set the tone for ministry in our groups. If discipled and equipped, *looking-for-ministry kids* will reach out to every kind of student in your group.

They begin going as missionaries to connect with their friends on the left side of the table. As they build relationships with *outreach students*, they will find opportunities to engage in spiritual conversations or invite them to venues where these conversations take place. Their investment in their friends' lives actually helps accomplish our purpose: Moving students to the right. I believe our *looking-for-ministry kids* are more effective at reaching their friends than we are. All they need is encouragement and help from us.

MENTORS

Our *looking-for-ministry kids* need mentors as much as any of our other types of students. They need encouragement, discipleship, and accountability. They need someone to ask tough questions when no one else does.

Looking-for-ministry kids are still learning to navigate their way through our R-rated culture with its celebrity-driven values. Even as we teach them biblical truth they are being barraged with "if it feels good" ethics (i.e., *How can it hurt you if it feels good?*).

We talked about it in the last two chapters—sometimes our "good church students" don't look much different than unchurched students.

In a podcast last year I asked my buddy Andy to bring two of his top student leaders to the studio so we could hear from them about service and missions. Andy brought two girls, Noelle and Sheah, both very bright students from good Christian homes—true *looking-for-ministry kids*. During a segment of the podcast called "Youth Culture Window," I discussed with these students the rise of cheating among today's teenagers. The starting point of our discussion was a recent survey that revealed 95 percent of teenagers admit to cheating.[xxiv]

The girls both shared about the enormous pressure to succeed and how that can drive students to feel the need to cheat just to keep up. I asked Noelle if church students were cheating just as much as unchurched students. I loved her answer. She said most church students have been taught what to do, and they know what's right. But then she concluded, "We know cheating is not right, but we still do it."

My friend Andy jumped in. "How did you feel the last time you did it?"

We chuckled at Andy's boldness. But Noelle was quick to reply. "Well, you do have a little bit of guilt, but sometimes when you cheat—it's to succeed. You feel like, *I have to do this*." She paused, "I don't know, it's hard to explain."

I walked away from that conversation with a greater understanding of our *looking-for-ministry kids*. Many of them still reflect some of the negative values and ethics of our society.

As mentors, we need to ask tough questions like these. *Why do you cheat?* Not to point fingers, but to seek understanding and help them navigate through the Scriptures for answers. These real-life experiences can be a catalyst for relevant and thought-provoking discussions. Our *looking-for-ministry kids* appreciate a focus on relevance. They desire to wrestle with the real issues of life and want your help in guiding them to apply God's wisdom in tough situations. Mentoring times with *discipleship students* can look like this:

1. **Start by each sharing your high and low of the week:** This is a meaningful exercise that gives each of you a chance to share something good and something challenging that happened during the week. It also gives each person a chance to understand a little more about the other person.

2. **Pray for each other:** Some people like to open in prayer. I like to pray after I know what's going on in the lives of the people in my group.

3. **Go over study materials:** Spend a little time studying, whether going through a discipleship book, a Christian book, or a book of the Bible. It's good to do this early on in the meeting so it doesn't get skipped.

4. **Ask goal-oriented questions:** Once you build a relationship with students, they usually want to share as well. Ask some well-thought-out questions to help the student share about life, relationships, and his or her spiritual walk.

Here are some questions you could ask:

- What is something you look forward to in the next year? Why?

- What is something you regret from the previous year?

- Who is your easiest friend to be good around? Why him/her?

- Which of your friends is it most difficult to be good around? Why him/her?

- What is one thing you did this week that demonstrated you are a Christian?

- What is one thing you did this week that made you hope those watching didn't know you were a follower of Christ?

- What characteristic or quality do you wish you had? Why?

- What do you think it would take for you to have that quality?

- How can I help you do this?

- Is there a question I'm not asking you I should be asking?

   I wouldn't necessarily ask all these questions every week, but they give you a good idea of the types of questions to ask. I usually start by asking about a victory before I ask about a failure. I also try to ask how I can help (e.g., the last two questions).

5. **Break Momentum:** Once every four to six weeks, blow off your normal discipleship venue and go do something just for fun. I took students on hikes, went to professional sports events, and had them over for dinner. But we mostly frequented an insanely good ice cream parlor by my house. *(Shout out to Leatherby's!)*

Mentor relationships are vital. When I ran the student ministry program at our church, I required every student to meet weekly with an adult mentor. This might sound like an intense requirement, but it was amazing how this connected our youth ministry with people in the church.

My son Alec went on a mission trip last year, and his youth pastor required every student attending the trip to connect with two adult prayer partners weekly for six weeks before the trip. These could be adults at church or elsewhere in the community. Alec chose his papa (my dad) and my good friend Tom, who also attends our church. Each Saturday Alec would go over to Papa's house and pray for the trip. On Sunday morning Alec would meet with Tom in the fellowship area between the buildings, sharing prayer requests, talking about his week, and praying. During these six weeks it was common to see as many as 20 groups of adults and students in the fellowship area praying together. This particular experience was huge for our students. I still meet students today who look back on it as one of the greatest helps in their Christian walk through high school.

STUDENT LEADERSHIP TEAMS

Often, youth leaders will find their ministries don't have many *looking-for-ministry kids*. They might have plenty of *growing kids* involved and growing in faith, but very few have moved to the right. These adult leaders always ask me, "How do I develop student leaders?"

I usually answer the question with another question. "Do you have a student-leadership team?" How are our students going to learn to minister to others if we don't provide opportunities to minister and serve? Sure, some students are going to look for ministry whether we provide opportunities or not, but most students could really use support, training, and encouragement in this area. One of the best ways we can do this is to start a student-leadership team.

Entire books have been written on developing student leaders—I'm co-writing one now with David R. Smith, a book focusing on developing ministry by students. I can't possibly cover everything in a few paragraphs, but here are a few points to consider:

SELECTING LEADERS

Don't just announce a student-leadership team and allow anyone to participate. Have an application process. (We provide a sample student-leadership application on our Web site at www.TheSource4YM.com on our Logistical Crud page.) Announce the team but also personally invite students you think should apply. The last team I led probably would have been half the size it was if I hadn't personally invited students. They didn't think they were "leadership material."

REQUIRE MENTORS

As detailed in the pages prior, I always require student leaders to meet weekly with adult mentors from our church body. This connects students with adults *one-on-one*, and it connects adults outside of our youth ministry with the youth in our church. (I also provide mentor applications on our Web site.)

TEAM BUILDING

I purposefully plan regular times for my student leaders to get together for fellowship, fun, and training. Whether your leadership team meets weekly or monthly, make sure you find a regular time to get together. One of the key ingredients you should include is team-building activities. (We provide a whole page of these types of activities on our Web site.)

Team-building activities accomplish two things. First, they can be a lot of fun. Sometimes student-leadership meetings can become pretty boring. Team-building activities add humor and build community in your group. Secondly, they allow an opportunity to actively learn together. As silly as some of these activities are, they really help students grow in the area of teamwork, patience, and problem solving. Furthermore, they include everyone. No student is left out. For some students, this can be one of the first positive team experiences in which they will ever participate.

EVANGELISM TRAINING

I've seen a myriad of subjects youth leaders use to teach their student leaders, many of them good. One area of equipping you should always include is evangelism training.

When I say evangelism training, I don't just mean teaching students how to use a tract. I do ask my students to memorize Scripture and be able to share their faith on the spot, but I also teach them the importance of their actions. I use passages like Matthew 5:16, 1 Peter 2:11-12, and 1 Peter 3:15-18 to talk about the importance of our actions creating opportunities to point to Jesus. I also teach them many of the same ideas we've been learning for mentoring: *Asking good questions, listening, caring for people's needs,* and *looking for opportunities to share.*

Student-leadership teams are a great way to focus specifically on equipping our *looking-for-ministry kids*.

SERVING

A *growing kid* and a *looking-for-ministry kid* might not seem very different—the main difference is serving. Our *looking-for-ministry kids* are already growing in faith, getting plugged into God's people, and being discipled. But now faith has become such a big part of life that it's overflowing to others, and they can't help but reach out.

We need to give them direction and provide service opportunities. This can be as simple as helping with a registration table at youth group or as immense as taking the role of student leader on a high school mission trip to Kenya.

Service projects are great for all types of students. I used to bring my *outreach students* on service projects. Simply serving does not make a student a *looking-for-ministry kid*. But a *looking-for-ministry kid* is always serving.

The best way to assess where students can best serve is by giving them a spiritual-gift test—gifts like mercy, faith, giving, and encouragement. Numerous books have been written on the subject, some providing detailed tests. Often, the lists of gifts will look like this:

Administration

Discernment

Faith

Giving

Hospitality

Knowledge

Leadership

Mercy

Prophecy

Helps/Service

Teaching

Wisdom

It's amazing to see what God does when we give people opportunities to serve in their areas of giftedness. But think about what happens when people serve in areas in which they are *not* gifted. Have you ever tried to listen to a talk given by a person who didn't have the gift of teaching?

Zzzzzzzzzzz.

Have you ever been to a party at someone's house who didn't have the gift of hospitality? Yeah, those experiences are pretty bad.

But contrast that to when a student discovers she has the gift of mercy, and you bring her to a homeless shelter to feed the hungry. You'll see a student be used by God in ways she's never been used before. The look on her face will say it all—she's empowered in a new way. If you don't have access to a spiritual-gift test, do an Internet search for "youth ministry spiritual-gift tests." I found thousands. Pick one you like that fits with your church's perspective on spiritual gifts.

LOOKING FOR MINISTRY

The *looking-for-ministry kids* want opportunities to use their gifts to make an impact. We have the awesome privilege of helping them do this. Provide mentors for these students, adults who are willing to disciple them and invest in them one-on-one. Start student -leadership teams, equipping these students and training them to reach out to non-Christians. Give them opportunities to serve. After all—they are looking for ministry.

We've looked at three different types of *discipleship students*, and we've seen how one-on-one time with these students can help them grow and engage in ministry. What does this actually look like? The following pages provide a glimpse of this process.

12

WHAT CONNECTING WITH *DISCIPLESHIP STUDENTS* LOOKS LIKE

PICTURE OF THE PROCESS

Outreach			Discipleship		
No Way	Not Interested	Checking Things Out	Stagnant	Growing	Looking for Ministry

The last three chapters were all about connecting with *discipleship students*. In all three chapters we saw the importance of getting to know our students, connecting with them one-on-one, discipling them, and plugging them in with God's people.

What does this actually look like?

I'm probably supposed to share a giant success story here—an encouraging anecdote about how I connected with a student and his life was changed forever. Instead, I'm going to share with you a story of how we failed.

I'll call him James. I've changed his name, but his story is very real—James is dear to my heart.

I met James when he was an *outreach student*. I did all the things we talked about in the outreach pages of this book. James came to Christ in a fast-food joint three minutes from his house and was immediately plugged into our church.

I started discipling James. We went through the *Welcome to the Family* book I often use. We talked about reading our Bible, praying, and the importance of a church family. James was excited about Christ. He went home and led his little sister to Christ; she began attending with James and got plugged into the church.

Before long they convinced their mom to attend our church. I sat down and shared the gospel with her several times—she thought it was great for us, but not for her.

James became very special to Lori and me. His mom was going through a rough divorce, and James and his sister were hurting. We often helped James' mother by taking care of James and his sister—sometimes for several days at a time.

James was growing in his faith through all of this. As a freshman he was already involved in the student-leadership team at the church and using his gifts to serve in the high school group.

I really respected James. I'll never forget a time when he and I were doing errands and we encountered a person who tried my patience. This person worked for a national truck-rental chain and was the rudest person I'd encountered in many years. As my temper began to flare, James looked up at me and simply said my name, "Jonathan." That's all he said, looking at me with an expression that said, *"Come on Jonathan. This isn't worth it. Back down."*

It's a humbling experience being rebuked by a 14-year-old.

James was incredibly mature. He loved God—he loved church. James was my prodigy. I thought for sure he'd become a pastor some day. But then we heard the news. James' mom got a job across the country.

I literally wept.

His mom was struggling with the whole move. She knew James was connected at school and church. Lori and I talked with her, and we actually discussed the possibility of James living with us. We sought out the advice of some wise family friends, and we decided it wouldn't be best for James or for us. I couldn't see James being split from his mom and his sister. Besides, Lori and I had just started our family. We had two children and another one on the way. We would have had to make some serious adjustments to "adopt" a teenager.

We prayed and prayed. I felt God leading us to let him go. As I discipled James, I knew time was short before they moved. I'd only had a little over a year with him. As much as he was growing, he was still a baby Christian. We read books together, even attended a Promise Keepers event together. I did everything I could to prepare him for the rapidly approaching transition.

We got on the phone and called churches in the town he'd be living. Through contact with a friend, we got the name of a good church in the area. I found the youth worker and had several conversations on the phone with her about James and his sister.

Soon, the move came. James' mom had left a week earlier, so my family took James and his sister to the airport. A lot of tears were shed that day.

At first, I checked in with James weekly. I even called the youth worker in his church to see how James was adjusting. James was pretty negative at first—he didn't like the church, and he had a list of things about the youth group he wished were different. We talked about his attitude and those shortcomings being opportunities for him to serve and make things better.

A year passed and our conversations and emails became less frequent. The church situation didn't get better, and James no longer wanted to talk about church, just wakeboarding and snowboarding. It was fun to talk about these things, but I grew concerned when he didn't want to talk about anything else.

Time passed and James' interest in the church faded. I'll never forget one conversation where James told me, "I just don't fit in there. I don't belong."

Even if students are engaged in worship and hear a great message at church, they miss a lot if they don't connect and build deep relationships. They long for a place where they can experience community—a place where their names and stories are known. They need a place that has people who care about them and will support them during tough times—a place where if you are missing... *you are missed.*

If our students don't find that at church, they'll seek to belong somewhere else. That's what happened to James. He bailed on church.

This broke my heart.

I keep in contact with James and his sister. James has a daughter now and lives with his girlfriend. We see his sister about once a year. Their mom is remarried, still living across the country.

I've replayed their situation over and over again in my mind. I've rethought it a thousand times. Should we have adopted James? What would have happened to his sister? Should we have adopted them both? Did we fail them? Did the church across the country fail?

I may never find answers to these questions, but I know one thing: James never connected in his new church. No one ever called up James and said, "Let me take you to lunch." "Let's go wakeboarding." "Let's go rent a truck."

No one met with James *one-on-one*. So a *looking-for-ministry kid* slowly digressed and became a *stagnant kid*. Now, I am not sure where James is spiritually. I try to visit him every time I am traveling near him, to show him I still love him.

Are you connecting with your *discipleship students?* Are you providing a place they can belong, a place where if you are missing... you are missed?

Don't let a "James" slip through your ministry. *Please.*

section four

CONNECTING AS A WAY OF LIFE AND MINISTRY

13
ONE-ON-ONE PRECAUTIONS AND BOUNDARIES

DISCLAIMER: Adults who want to spend one-on-one time with students are under great scrutiny today. We'd be foolish not to set boundaries and guidelines to protect the people we minister to and our ministries. Please consult your leadership, your organization, and/or your denomination for advice in regard to setting boundaries and guidelines and taking precautions in regard to relational ministry.

Scott led a growing youth ministry near my house. "All students need is a mentor," he'd say. Scott was a hero in the community. He reached out to the unlovable. The tougher the student, the more he extended love and attention. Scott would receive phone calls at all hours of the night: "Can you come get me? Things are really bad. I need someone to talk to." It didn't matter to Scott or his wife Amy who it was—girl or boy—Scott would be there. "Go get her," Amy would encourage Scott. "She needs you."

It was common to see Scott give rides and spend time at lunch or dinner with teenage girls. Many perceived Scott as a big brother, but youth ministry peers warned him, "Scott, you can't take a teenage girl to lunch."

"Why not?" Scott would ask, frustrated with what our society had become. "I'm the only adult in her life who seems to care about her."

Scott wouldn't listen. Whenever he brought up the subject to Amy, she was supportive of his time with the teenagers. "I trust you Scott. I know what a good man you are, and that's all that matters."

Before long, a girl accused Scott of sexual misconduct and some inappropriate pictures were found on his computer. In a long, drawn-out trial, the defense attorney argued Scott didn't know about the pictures. "Others had access to this computer."

It didn't matter. Too many people had seen Scott at numerous locations alone with the girl who made the accusations. When the verdict was read, some of the jury members were in tears. "I really think he was a good man. But even good men fail."

Scott wouldn't take the deal and admit his guilt. "I didn't do it," he maintained. "I don't care what kind of reduced sentence they offer me. I'm not going to admit to something I didn't do."

Scott's wife Amy and his close friends maintain he's innocent. Scott's life has been changed forever. He is facing hundreds of thousands of dollars in court fees, a jail sentence, and a blotch on his record that will never be removed. Guilty or not, Scott didn't set appropriate boundaries.

Think of your own ministry. Could someone accuse you of failing to set appropriate boundaries? Could you easily end up in a situation where it would be a student's word against yours?

I've met hundreds of youth workers who believe they are immune to accusation and temptation. To them, *the ends justify the means.* They don't want to be restricted by stupid boundaries that seem to limit their interaction with students.

Take a moment and go to www.BadBadTeacher.com. Every day you'll see a new teacher or youth worker now blacklisted for a variety of offenses. Some have just been arrested and await trial while others have already been found guilty. As I glanced at the site today, I saw the following top stories:

- A 34-year-old male, a Pennsylvania chemistry teacher, has been arrested in an Internet sex sting.

- A 25-year-old male, a former youth pastor and teacher's aide, accused of molesting four boys.

- A 30-year-old male, a girls' basketball coach from Missouri, has been charged with second-degree statutory rape of a 16-year-old female.

- A 28-year-old female teacher from California has been found guilty of having oral sex with a minor.

No wonder our society is growing skeptical of adults who show care for students. When it comes to my own children—I'm growing skeptical. Let's be honest—the titles *reverend, priest,* and *pastor* don't elicit the trust they used to.

A youth worker named Tonya wrote me with this story:

> Recently we took our students on a camping trip to Lake Erie. The volatile weather in that part of Ohio foiled our beach plans, sending us all dashing to the van to head back to the campground. Once at the campground, we realized that one of our youngest students, "Austin" (age 12), left his flip-flops at the beach. Everybody exited the van, and my husband and son were busy building a fire while Austin searched frantically through everybody's stuff in the van for his flip-flops—which, as it turned out,

were the only shoes he brought, and it was pouring down rain.

Feeling a bit stressed out, I drove off with Austin, completely forgetting about our "nobody is ever alone for any reason" rule. It didn't even occur to me at the moment that had my husband been driving off with one of the girls, it would have been completely inappropriate. However, I was soon snapped back into reality when Austin made a disturbing comment en route to the beach."Where are we going?" he asked. "This isn't the way to the beach, is it?"

"Yes", I replied, "it just looks different because it got darker out."

Austin shifted uncomfortably in his seat. "Oh," he replied.

Suddenly I realized he seemed somewhat afraid. "Why do you ask?" I said.

"Oh—because you know—there are perverts."

My heart sunk as the full realization of my snap decision hit me. Austin was 12 years old, three hours from home, and had been lectured about molestation before he left. He didn't know the area, and so he thought I was taking him somewhere else.

I'll never forget the look on his face. That probably felt like a very long ride. Boy was he glad when we fetched his shoes and returned to camp with everyone else.

Parents and students alike are becoming more and more suspicious of once-trusted adults. They have watched the news and *Dateline* specials devoted to this volatile issue.

In fact, as I'm writing this chapter (how's that for timing?), I just received the following phone call from my son's high school:

> This morning before school a parent reported an adult male was seen performing a sexual act in his car in the vicinity of the high school (my son's school).
>
> The following message was sent to our students this afternoon during fourth period: Please be cautious while walking to and from school. I'd strongly advise you not to talk to a stranger, and most certainly do not accept rides from anyone who you do not know personally. If you are confronted by a stranger going to and from school, be sure to report the incident to the administration office as soon as possible.

Obviously the person doing this is disturbed. But people like this are making it more and more difficult for trusted adults to spend time with students. In many settings, adult mentoring programs are at risk of becoming extinct.

So should we abandon everything we've learned in this book? After all, *one-on-one* sounds pretty scary in today's world.

Give up? Absolutely not. I am still a firm believer in the power of one-on-one relationships, but we are foolish if we think boundaries and guidelines are unnecessary. We need to protect the students in our community, and we need to do our best to protect ourselves and our ministries from accusation.

I am not a lawyer, and I cannot offer you any legal advice. But I do hope to offer you some commonsense principles that might help as you consider using one-on-one time as a tool to reach out to students.

SCREENING

One of the most important practices ministries should employ is a background check of every person who has interaction with minors.

Most of you who have volunteered at a school or as a coach have probably had a background check. When my wife and I signed up to help at my youngest daughter's elementary school, we filled out an application giving permission for a background check, then we drove to the local sheriff's office to be fingerprinted.

We experienced the same procedure when we worked with the junior high group at our church. Be prepared to face adults who believe background checks are inconvenient and unneeded. One year I had to have three background checks for three different entities where I volunteered. By the third one I was thinking, "Can't they just use the results from my last two background checks—*last month.*"

But a little inconvenience is well worth it. Churches are improving but still seem the most relaxed about screening adults. Predators know this about churches, and many still use churches to target children.

Fingerprinting and background checks are necessary protections. Without them, churches named in lawsuits have nothing to provide a judge regarding why they let registered sex offenders volunteer with children and youth.

My dad recently served as an interim pastor for a local church and used www.ChurchVolunteerCentral.com for all their staff and volunteer background checks. He said it was well worth the money and demonstrated to his congregation they care about the safety of their children and adults.

ONE-ON-ONE PRECAUTIONS AND BOUNDRIES

BOUNDARIES

I see five major boundaries youth workers should put into practice:

Gender Boundaries

Gender boundaries are this simple: Men only invest one-on-one time with other males, women only invest one-on-one time with females. Obviously this does not prevent inappropriate same-gender contact, but it is a good starting point that may protect you from a majority of issues.

Recently, while teaching a seminar, I met Todd, a 21-year-old junior high pastor at a small church. He had been an exemplary student leader in his youth group, so when he decided to go to college locally, the church was quick to hire him as part-time junior high pastor.

Each Sunday, the high school and junior high youth groups met together. That's where he met Rebecca, who was 15 (going on 19). They hit it off right away, and soon Todd and Rebecca were being seen together often.

The church didn't have a policy about guys mentoring guys and girls mentoring girls. So Todd simply argued, "I'm helping her through some tough times."

Then one of the junior highers saw Todd kissing Rebecca on the church's Mexico trip.

When Rebecca's parents found out what "the church had allowed to happen," they threatened litigation.

People—especially males—will take great risks for a quick moment of pleasure. Lives are ruined by people following their sexual desires. We see in our world:

- Ministers having to leave the ministry because of porn addictions

- Priests breaking their vows of celibacy to feed sexual urges

- Pastors losing their ministries and marriages because of affairs

- Important political leaders risking their reputations for one moment of pleasure

- Fathers risking their families for acts of infidelity

- The pornography industry growing by leaps and bounds based on huge demand

Yet some people still believe we should allow a man to meet with a young, attractive 17-year-old girl, listening to her innermost thoughts and providing comfort as she shares her deep feelings. *This is a BIG problem.*

I will not meet with a teenage girl one-on-one, period. Not only would my wife kill me, but it's just not appropriate. I don't counsel girls or give them rides home (even if it's inconvenient).

Churches definitely disagree on these kinds of policies.

For example, take Tina's description of her church's policy:

> We have a very strict child-protection policy. We are not allowed to meet with students under the age of 18 alone. We MUST meet in a public place where other people are present. If we meet in the church or somewhere someone else isn't present, there must be at least two students or two adults. We are not allowed to drive alone with only one student in the car. It is highly suggested that we meet with same-gender students, but not a requirement (thank goodness).

Tina's church obviously set boundaries about age, setting, and number of people present. But they don't have gender boundaries, only advice.

If it were up to me, every church would incorporate gender boundaries. With gender and other appropriate boundaries (like meeting in public places), we can help create safe environments for one-on-one mentoring—something Tina's church doesn't allow right now.

Meeting Boundaries

Meeting boundaries should encompass everywhere you spend time with a student, including car rides. I like that Tina's policy (above) requires meeting in a public place. Public places create safety. Why do you think dating Web sites and social-networking sites always tell people to meet in public places?

This boundary does create some restrictions when it comes to *one-on-one* time. No overnight trips and no hanging out at the house playing Xbox. The tough situation this rule brings up is driving. For many ministries, giving students rides is a huge factor. Students often need rides, And if you can't have one student in your car alone, that makes things very difficult. In the past I allowed my volunteers to pick up and drop off students (of the same gender) alone. But some ministries draw the line at "no place alone, including a car." I respect that. It might mean a student finding his or her own ride to meet you for some one-on-one time. Or it might mean you bringing your spouse and children along, then grabbing another booth with the student for some one-on-one time.

Media Boundaries

Numerous ministries have policies about seeing R-rated films and playing M-rated (mature) games. A growing number of churches are also creating policies about contact with students on the Internet and cell phones.

I recently read a CNN article titled, "Online Student-Teacher Friendships Can Be Tricky."[xxv]

The article detailed the state of Missouri's response to 11 teachers arrested and convicted of inappropriate behavior with students in the last two years. The articles pointed to social-networking sites as a factor in the inappropriate student-teacher relationships, leading to a bill in the Missouri House of Representatives that would ban elementary school teachers from having social-networking friendships with their students.

The same article cited an example in which a mom thought a teacher was giving her child some needed extra attention, helping the child overcome shyness. The parents eventually checked the child's phone bill and found 4,200 text messages between the teacher and student.

It's sad to see some of these technologies abused. Last year I led a small group of junior high boys and I found texting them was the best way to keep in touch throughout the week. Texting helped me check in with them and plan face-to-face meetings. It would be sad if texting becomes banned between adults and teenagers.

I've also found social-networking sites helpful in connecting with teens. A Facebook page for my group helped us stay connected and plan times together with the click of a button. Facebook or similar sites are simply springboards I've used to facilitate connections with my students.

When using social-networking sites, texting, or even email, make sure you use extreme discretion. I've seen others in ministry make costly mistakes by being careless with the use of media. Here are a few commonsense tips when using media to connect with students:

- Never type anything to a student you wouldn't be comfortable with their parents, your pastor, or your spouse reading.

- Never promote an arena of technology that can lure students into temptations that didn't exist before you introduced that arena (e.g., don't tell students who weren't already on MySpace to get a MySpace page. On MySpace they can easily click *browse* and see hundreds of girls in their area wearing very little clothing).

- Never encourage students to use technology at an inappropriate time. For example: Texting students during school if you know they aren't allowed to use cell phones during school hours—or contacting students in the middle of the night.

Connecting with students through the use of technology is such a new medium for many churches that boundaries are just now being discussed. Any time you sense your communication with a student is going in an unhealthy direction, seek accountability from your spouse and your church leadership.

Family Boundaries

As youth workers, we need to make extra efforts to respect a student's time with family.

I've worked with students from wonderful homes and with some in such terrible circumstances I needed to contact Child Protective Services. Regardless of the quality of their home lives, we need to help students respect their families and be careful to support the growth of family relationships.

As I look back on my ministry a decade ago, I think I overstepped family boundaries on numerous occasions, particularly with some of my students from unhealthy homes. I swooped in and "saved" these unfortunate students from alcoholic and unstable parents. What I didn't realize was I was providing an easy escape for some of these students from already wobbly relationships. Mentoring students is unarguably beneficial, but pulling students away from their homes too much could drive a deep wedge in the relationship between parents and children.

Don't get me wrong. In cases of abuse (verbal or physical), the best thing for a student is to get proper authorities involved. But placing ourselves in competition with parents or in the middle of family crises is a mistake. Chances are, parents will be in the lives of their kids longer than you.

So how can we engage in relationships with students and avoid hurting or stealing time from family relationships?

MEET FAMILIES

The powerful film *Dangerous Minds* (1995) stars Michelle Pfeifer as LouAnne Johnson, a new teacher who makes a difference in an inner-city school. Whenever I watch the film, one scene always strikes me: The moment when the teacher decides to go beyond the walls of the campus and visit some of the students' homes.

When LouAnne knocks on Raul's door, the mother answers it skeptically. When she finds out LouAnne is Raul's teacher, the mother quickly responds, "What has he done now?" Then, Pfeifer's character basically tells the mother, "Your son is a joy to have in the classroom." The tension breaks and everyone relaxes at this good news. This springboards a relationship between Ms. Johnson and Raul.

But the film takes a turn of realism I could relate to, having worked in tough neighborhoods. LouAnne ventures out on more home visits, soaring on the encouragement of her earlier successes. As she approaches the house of another student, she is verbally assaulted by the mother. LouAnne is shocked. The sharp contrast between appreciation and resentment is brilliantly portrayed, a disturbing reality many youth workers experience.

Our encounters with families aren't always going to be positive. But they are necessary. As we strive to invest in students one-on-one, we need to be proactive about meeting families and gaining their trust. For many families, trust must be earned, not freely given. I can assure you as a parent of an elementary-aged girl, a junior high girl, and a high school boy, I wouldn't let any of them spend time with someone who's a stranger to me.

Meeting our students' parents can open doors to incredible family ministry opportunities, which brings up the second area we can be proactive about—respecting family boundaries.

EXTEND YOUR MINISTRY TO INCLUDE FAMILIES

Youth ministry is less than a century old. The first professional youth worker is no older than my dad. The Sunday "youth service" is younger than me. In perspective, separating youth and adults in church is a recent trend. And I am not sure this approach is a good one.

I've been to several churches where parents wave goodbye to their children at 8:45 a.m. Sunday morning and don't see them again until a few minutes after noon. We have separate services and separate fellowship groups—even if we're in the same service, we don't sit together.

Follow this logic. We separate youth culture and adult culture for 22 years. Then upon graduation from college, students are expected to immediately blend with the adults they've been separated from for 22 years. No wonder these young generations feel the need to start churches of their own. They've never been taught how to have relationships with anyone more than three years older than themselves.

Perhaps we should consider keeping the family together more often in our ministries. Maybe we should extend our outreach events to entire families?

I'm not alone in this thinking. The term *Family-Based Youth Ministry*[xxvi] grew popular in the 1990s, introducing ministry methodologies that tried to swing the pendulum back toward a family-centered ministry model. Perhaps we should initiate programs where the whole family can attend?

While I'm not seeking to write a book on Family-Based Youth Ministry, I do hope our ministries would consider incorporating opportunities that bring families together. I'm not saying you need to get rid of youth night and call it family night—just that we find ways to involve the whole family on a more regular basis.

When I worked with unchurched students, part of my ministry was bringing them to church. I didn't limit that invitation to students. As I met different families in my community, I was able to extend the invitation to entire families.

And I began to notice something: The students who began attending with their families (as a result of my invite) became regular attendees at a much higher rate than those students I brought alone. This really isn't surprising if you think about it. The students who relied on rides from me didn't go unless I went. If I was out of town speaking at a camp, they didn't go. Sadly, in many of those cases, I was their only connection to the church. But the families that attended together were much more successful at getting connected.

Don't ignore the opportunity to reach the entire family. Throw holiday parties for families. Have regular events involving parents. If you need some ideas, we have some fun games on our Web site that are challenges between parents and students.

Note: Realize this world is full of split families. If you host an event that is exclusive, like a Daddy-Daughter Banquet, consider the feelings of the girl who has no father in her life. When we plan and promote our events, we must be sensitive to the fact that many families today are broken.

Personal Boundaries

A lot of young youth workers make the mistake of not guarding their own family times. I know I've experienced this firsthand. We begin to confuse our relationship with God and our ministry to students as equally important. A Christian zookeeper doesn't have this same dilemma—his priority list might look like this:

1. God

2. Family

3. Friends

4. My job shoveling monkey poop

5. Hobbies

Etc.

A youth worker's list often becomes this:

1. God/ministry

2. Family

3. Friends

4. Hobbies

5. Preparation for my divorce hearing on Monday

With youth workers, family often slips to the back burner behind ministry. "Sorry, honey, duty calls." "Sorry, cutey. I'd love to, but I've got a junior higher who really needs someone to talk to."

Wake up. Your *spouse* needs someone to talk to. Your *family* is more important than your ministry to students.

A little over a decade ago, my messed-up priorities began affecting my marriage. My wife was tired of me abandoning our family for "urgent" ministry duties. She took our children and was heading out the door. I literally got on my knees and pleaded with her to stay. I was spending quality time with all my volunteers, leaving slim to none for my wife. I was hanging out with students whose parents had neglected them—but I was no different, as I was neglecting my own children. As my wife headed for the door, I opened my daily planner (back in the Stone Age, before it was electronic) and laid it on the floor in front of her. I begged her to look at the planner and simply tell me what to change. I handed her a pen saying, "You cross it out, and I'll cancel it."

Thankfully, she stayed, and things changed. I sought counsel from several pastors, and they all said the same thing: "Stop trying to do everything yourself. You need to develop people who can help you carry this load." We created a "date night" that took first priority. My volunteers knew which night that was, and they respected it. My (then) seven-pound, brick-shaped cell phone (remember those?) was turned off that night. Family night grew from that experience. I began to learn to delegate better, and I became a better time manager.

Don't make the mistakes I did. Don't let ministry become more important than your own family.

GUARD YOURSELF

If these five boundaries seem stifling, I challenge you to reevaluate your perspective. They are not meant to confine you; they are meant to be sentinels protecting and empowering you toward healthy ministry.

You aren't bulletproof. I know Superman personally, and you are not him.

Guard yourself. You, your family, your ministry, and God deserve it.

14

INSTILLING THE VALUE OF ONE-ON-ONE IN YOUR MINISTRY

"I just wonder if we're really making a difference."

Those were the words Phil used to describe his youth ministry. Phil had been at a small church for five years. About 20 to 25 students attended the Wednesday-night youth program each week. The parents thought he was doing a great job, but Phil questioned his effectiveness.

"I guess I would just like to see some fire in the eyes of these students," Phil confessed. "They seem complacent. They come to youth group because there's nothing else to do. They get fired up at summer camp every year, but it only lasts a few weeks."

I've heard the exact same thing from youth workers around the country. Phil pleaded with me, "Is there anything I can do?"

Can you guess my response?

I asked him the question: "Are you and your adult leaders spending time with students one-on-one?"

And that's when Phil really earned my respect. He didn't give excuses; he stopped and truly pondered the question for a moment. I could almost see his mental gears turning as he thought through every aspect of his ministry, considering where they created opportunities for one-on-one conversation; *Sunday mornings, Wednesday nights, small groups, events...* He had chaperones. He had volunteers who talked to students on Wednesday nights—but that wasn't what I'd asked. I'd asked if Phil and his leaders were spending time with students one-on-one.

Finally, he answered honestly, "Not really."

I appreciated Phil's candidness. Whenever I ask this question to youth leaders, I usually hear a myriad of different responses (or should I say, excuses):

"I've never been that strong relationally."

"I'm more of a program guy."

"My leaders are too busy. I can hardly get them to come on Wednesday nights."

"We use small groups instead."

"My pet monkey Reggie just died—I'm really torn up about it."

Phil didn't use any of these excuses. Instead he just asked me, "Do you really think it would make a difference?"

Three months later I was at Phil's church training his volunteer leaders. I taught them about today's youth culture and introduced the six types of students. We brainstormed how to go outside of the church walls to reach out to students in the community. We also discussed how some outreach programming could create first contact for some of these *outreach students.*

Phil and his volunteer leaders inventoried their youth group students, writing their names on the *six-types-of-students* table we've used in this book. Then they discussed specific goals for each leader and each student.

Phil also made a budget decision that day. He invested in $30 gift cards from a local coffee shop for each of his volunteers. His instructions: "We value your one-on-one time with students. Use this card any time you're out with students one-on-one. I'll refill the card when it's empty."

Phil and his leaders began investing in the lives of students face-to-face, one student at a time. These students began to connect and grow in faith. *Stagnant kids* became *growing kids, growing kids* became *looking-for-ministry kids*, and *looking-for-ministry kids* began bringing their friends—both *checking-things-out kids* and even a few *not-interested kids*.

Phil's group wasn't just growing in size; his students were growing to be more like Jesus.

Tamara, a youth leader, didn't know any *no-way* or *not-interested kids*. She began attending the weekly high school girls' soccer games where one of her volunteers, Carol, was an assistant coach. The two of them met several *not-interested kids* on the team as well as a *no-way kid* named Haley. Tamara and Carol built relationships with these students over the next year and eventually brought most the team, including Haley, to the church's Christmas Eve service. Haley didn't fall on her knees and pray right there in the aisle, but she did share with Carol she might have been wrong about church.

Then, Haley began attending youth group with Carol after soccer practice on Wednesday nights.

It's funny when I reflect on these situations. Both Phil and Tamara didn't change their programming much. Sundays remained the same; Wednesday nights weren't restructured. With the exception of a new student-leadership program, the programming in their ministries hardly changed. But now students in both ministries were growing in faith and becoming involved in service. Student leaders were being developed, and both groups were growing in numbers, because students and adult leaders were going beyond the church walls to reach out to students in the community.

The big difference in these ministries was that leaders made one-on-one time a priority with students. Their team meetings emphasized this, their budget reflected this (including a sizable coffee-shop bill), and their student-leadership programs taught it. Students were being invested in one at a time, and that made all the difference in the world.

APPLYING ONE-ON-ONE TO YOUR MINISTRY

Some of you might feel like Phil. You're working hard, but you wonder if you're really making an impact.

Have you tried making *one-on-one* a priority?

Notice I didn't ask if you connect with students *every once in a while*. I asked if you've made meeting with students *one-on-one* a priority.

Did Someone Say Training?

In chapter two of this book I quote authors, speakers, and professors who all agree on the importance of connecting with students in our ministries. Mark Oestreicher expanded on this by suggesting, *"I think all volunteers need basic training on how to connect with teenagers."*

Once we understand the importance of relational ministry, we need to do something about it. That usually begins with motivating our volunteers and training them how to connect with teenagers.

Each summer before the school year began, I planned a weekend retreat for all my adult ministry leaders (volunteers). This retreat was full of fun activities, great food, and a good amount of training. The training varied year to year with topics shifting from youth culture to ministry methodology to evangelism. But every year, without exception, I trained my staff how to connect with students one-on-one.

Whether you plan a weekend retreat, a Saturday training, or a quick two-hour training workshop after church on Sunday, make this training a priority. Get your youth leaders together and equip them to connect with the students your ministry is trying to reach.

Maybe you're thinking: *But I don't know how to train leaders. I wouldn't know what to do.*

I knew some of you were going to wonder about that. Which is why I'm going to provide you with a step-by-step guide with teaching, discussion, and activities that will help your staff connect with students in your ministry. Feel free to customize this to fit your ministry and teaching style.

SEVEN STEPS TO TEACHING YOUR LEADERS TO CONNECT

STEP 1: Motivate Your Leaders to Own It

You may be convinced of the power of *one-on-one*, but now you need to help your leaders understand the importance of this kind of relational ministry. You need to instill the value of *one-on-one* in your ministry from the very beginning. This starts with recruiting adults who want to be more than uninvolved chaperones. You need adults who want to connect with students.

When I first recruited my leaders, I always let them know the most important priority in our ministry was hanging out with students *one-on-one*. I talk about this in my book about recruiting, managing, and training volunteers, *The New Breed* (Group 2007). As I met with potential volunteers and talked to them about my ministry, I fully disclosed that I wasn't interested in mere chaperones. The information and application I provided to potential volunteers clearly stated the top priority in our ministry was connecting caring adults with students *one-on-one*. (See "Volunteer Expectations" in the appendix of this book. Please feel free to use it in your own ministry.)

Some of you might be wondering, *What if I already have a bunch of existing leaders who are comfortable with just being chaperones? How do I challenge them to be more involved with students?*

Here are some ways to help your volunteers capture the importance of connecting with students:

- *Invite someone to train your youth leaders about the importance of relational ministry.* Our ministry at www.TheSource4YM.com provides these kinds of trainers. We even have a training seminar called "Connect," during which we teach the principles from this book to volunteers and staff.

- *Train your leaders yourself.* Create your own training outline from chapter two of this book, teaching your youth leaders the power of one-on-one relationships.

- *Give each of your leaders a copy of this book.* Read it as a team, and then discuss it at a designated time. Talk about how your ministry can make connecting with students a priority.

- *Meet with your leaders one-on-one* and go over a "volunteer expectations" sheet similar to the one I've included in the appendix. Have a discussion with them about the importance of "hanging out" with and investing in students.

As you can see, there are numerous ways to instill the value of *one-on-one* in your ministry. You can train your team as a group or individually. Whatever method you use, training is essential.

STEP 2: Understand Outreach Versus Discipleship

Once my leaders understand the priority of *one-on-one*, I make sure they also understand the difference between *outreach* and *discipleship* ministry. With some groups, this might only take a few minutes.

You can use my definitions to help explain this: *Outreach* is connecting with people who don't know Jesus and pointing them to him through words and actions. *Discipleship* is helping believers grow closer to Jesus and live more like him.

Outreach	Discipleship

Draw a diagram like the one shown and begin asking for examples of both *outreach* and *discipleship* ministry with students. Hopefully, your leaders will come up with examples that match the definitions you've provided for outreach and discipleship. If they try to force something into the wrong category, go back to the definition for clarification. For example, if someone suggests Wednesday night choir practice is outreach, simply ask them if choir practice does what our definition of outreach suggests, i.e., "helping those who don't know Jesus to find him through our words and actions."

(If you are new to this kind of thinking, I discuss a definition of outreach along with numerous examples in two of my previous books, *Getting Students to Show Up* and *Do They Run When They See You Coming?* These books might be good resources to familiarize yourself with before embarking on this conversation with your leaders.)

Once your team understands the difference between *outreach* and *discipleship* ministry, then it's time to take a peek at the different types of students they will encounter.

STEP 3: Recognize the Six Types of Students

Describe the six types of students your workers will encounter.

Use the *six-types-of-students* table to help your workers visualize what the students look like in your ministry. (I've included a blank one you can copy in the appendix.) You may even want to use examples of students from your ministry.

Chapter four provides a great overview of all six types of students. You may want to give your volunteers a copy of this book so they can read about the six types of students they will encounter. Meet and discuss what you've read. Talk about how what you've read applies to your ministry.

Once your leaders understand the difference between *outreach* and *discipleship* ministry and are introduced to the six types of students—then it's time to get together as a leadership team and inventory your students.

STEP 4: Inventory Your Students

At this point you should've accomplished the following:

STEP 1: Recruited volunteer leaders who understand the priority of one-on-one relationships in your ministry. They understand you want to connect adults with students.

STEP 2: Taught your leaders the difference between *outreach* and *discipleship* ministry.

STEP 3: Introduced the six types of students they will encounter.

Now it's time to apply this knowledge to your ministry.

Student Inventory Exercise: This is a fun activity I always enjoy doing with my volunteer leaders at a training workshop or retreat. *(It is important this activity is done with just your adult leaders. You'll be talking about specific students—not something you should be doing in front of other students.)*

Use a flipchart, a big whiteboard, or even a big piece of butcher paper tacked on a wall. (I prefer to use a big piece of paper that can be rolled up and saved.)

Draw a vertical line down the middle of the page and write *outreach* on the left side and *discipleship* on the right. Then write the *six types of students* underneath with vertical lines dividing each student. The result should look like the following *six-types-of-students* table we've used throughout the book:

Outreach			Discipleship		
No Way	Not Interested	Checking Things Out	Stagnant	Growing	Looking for Ministry

Now, give each of your adult leaders a pad of normal-sized sticky notes and a bold marker. They will need as many sticky notes as the number of students they know.

Tell your leaders to write on a sticky note the names of *all* the students they know or are in contact with, one name per sticky note. Make sure you remind them to write down names of students they have regular contact with, even if they don't attend youth group on a consistent basis. Instruct them to write these names in large, legible print. If your adults are small group leaders, then they can write out one sticky note for every student in their small groups. If the students they know are just students they see on Sundays or midweek, that's fine, too. The object is to try to get the name of every student in your ministry on a sticky note.

If your ministry is new to the concept of connecting with students, it's always interesting to see which students your leaders know. This exercise tends to reveal how little we do know about our students.

If you don't have students designated with specific leaders, then this becomes really interesting to see the overlap. I've seen ministries in which every leader had a sticky note with the same student's name on it and numerous students unaccounted for.

Who's that student with the short dark hair who always wears that Guitar Hero shirt and sits in the back?

In my ministry each of my volunteer leaders were asked to find at least five same-gender students they would be responsible for. These kids would be the five students they would seek to build relationships with and invest in. When our leaders met every Wednesday night, we would each share how our "five kids" were doing.

Back to the exercise. Once your leaders have written names on the sticky notes, have them come up to the front of the room, one at a time, and place those sticky notes on the big *six-types-of-students* table you have on the wall. Have them provide the reasoning of why they think that particular student belongs in that category. Then ask the other adults if they agree or disagree with where that student was placed. This can create a lively discussion.

"Did Michael ever accept Christ?"

"I don't know. I assumed so. He's at church every week."

"Yeah, but maybe he's a *not-interested kid* who is forced to come each week."

"But the way he talks in our small group time, I think he's made a commitment at one time or another. He's definitely *not interested* — but I think he's a *stagnant* kid."

These discussions are great. First, they reveal how much we *don't* know about Michael. Secondly, they pave the way to goals we can make in our time with Michael. *(We don't know if Michael has made a decision or not, but either way he seems uninterested. So let's try to build a relationship with him, discover his needs, and engage in spiritual conversations.)*

Have every one of your leaders place their sticky notes on the *six-types-of-students* chart. Then, take a moment and determine if there are students who aren't on this chart. If you have a list of students who attend your group, maybe read down the list and see if all the students are accounted for. Don't place any student on the chart if you don't have an idea where they belong. Place those students on another chart labeled "Unknown." This separate chart might be a good starting place for some of the students you want to reach out to. After all, these students have been slipping in and out "under the radar." None of your leaders know them. Try to change that.

Once you've completed your inventory, step back and take a good look at your *six-types-of-students* table.

STEP 5: Notice Trends

It's amazing how much you can learn about your ministry simply from analyzing the location of sticky notes on a piece of butcher paper.

Let's look at a couple of examples to help us identify some trends:

EXAMPLE 1: CALVARY CHURCH

Outreach			Discipleship		
No Way	Not Interested	Checking Things Out	Stagnant	Growing	Looking for Ministry
		Morgan T.J.	David Nate Alyssa Zach Brandon	Tyler Michelle Dillon Amy Rebecca	Lisa Drew

What do you notice about this group?

The first thing you probably notice is this ministry is doing a lot of discipleship, but hardly any outreach. The table doesn't lie. If you don't know any *outreach students*, how are you supposed to reach out to them?

If your table looks like example one, then you might have to ask yourself, *Where can I meet some* no-way *and* not-interested kids? Maybe reread chapters five and six and develop a strategic plan to meet teens in these categories.

Take another look at example one. Do you notice another deficit?

Yep, this group has only two students in the *looking-for-ministry* column. So even though they have numerous students who are growing in faith *(growing kids)*, they really haven't begun to develop them into spiritual leaders who are using their gifts, serving, and reaching out to others. That very well could be another reason the left-hand side of the table is empty—the students are doing the exact same thing as their youth pastor: Ignoring *outreach students.*

EXAMPLE 2: RIVERDALE COMMUNITY CHURCH

Outreach			Discipleship		
No Way	Not Interested	Checking Things Out	Stagnant	Growing	Looking for Ministry
R.J. Matt	Kelly Jenny Laticia Micah	Lisa Heather Jamail Mike Melissa	James Brandon Kate Nathan Ricky	Tyler	

What do you notice about this group?

First of all, this ministry is doing a good job finding *outreach students.* But what are they doing with them? Are any of them coming to Christ? More so, are any of those new Christians being discipled and growing in faith?

I ran an on-campus outreach ministry for a decade, so I'm not going to be too quick to throw stones at this ministry. *Outreach* ministry is very difficult. But one of the ongoing struggles I had to face in my *outreach* ministry was responsible evangelism. What good are we really doing if we aren't making disciples?

Effective *outreach* ministry will see kids being moved to the right on this *six-types-of-students* table.

Now, step back, look at your own chart, and discuss the following questions with your leaders:

Notice the types of students your ministry is effectively reaching. Why do you think this is? What relational efforts are contributing to this? What programs are contributing to this?

Notice the types of students your ministry is *missing. Why do you think this is?* How might we need to change our relational efforts and programs to reach these types of students?

As you step back and look at the entire table, ask, *What does it tell us about our youth ministry?*

How might we become a more balanced ministry?

How can you—the adult leaders—help accomplish this?

How might the students in our ministry help us accomplish this?

How can I (we) show unconditional love to each student we have contact with?

It's important for us to remember that the work of ministry is very personal. It's all about relationships and investment in young lives. So regardless of where students land on our chart, we must be committed to love and serve them as Christ would.

STEP 6: Programming for Balance

This book is about relational ministry, but programming—or what we do in our ministry—often provides us with the first contact needed for relational ministry.

We need to create opportunities that put us in contact with all six types of students. Sometimes students come to us, but very often, we must go to them.

PROGRAMMING AFFECTS OUR POPULATION

Take an honest look at your ministry's programming and your daily activities as a youth worker for a moment. Use the same table I introduced at the beginning of the chapter and write down every activity, event, program, or ministry effort you and your ministry have tried in the last three to six months. After all, everything we do can easily be divided into one of these two categories: *Outreach* or *discipleship*.

Do you have a Wednesday-night program? Write it down where applicable. Do you have a Bible study? Write it down. Do you visit on campus? Write it down—it's a ministry effort.

This exercise could reveal something common in youth ministry. Our programming and ministry efforts usually favor one column.

It might look something like this.

Outreach	Discipleship
Battle of the Bands	Sunday School
	Wednesday Night
	Bible Studies
	Small Groups
	"Big Church"

I've given this exercise to youth workers across the U.S. and found most churches are stuck on one side of the chart or the other—few have found balance in their ministries.

Look at the example. This youth ministry is stuck in the right column. They still have Sunday school on Sunday mornings. Maybe they call it something else, but its purpose is definitely spiritual growth for those who are already Christians (they're currently studying Abraham's journey from Haran).

Wednesday nights usually go like this: *Hang out for 15 minutes, play a few games, worship for 25 minutes, and then listen to a 25-minute talk.* Even though a few students bring their friends, the focus is spiritual growth. The vast majority—98 percent—of Bible studies are focused on spiritual growth. This ministry is one of the 98 percent.

For this ministry, the small groups are also focused on spiritual growth. They are using a curriculum about using spiritual gifts.

And don't forget "Big Church" (that's what a lot of us call it). Teenage students go to the main service, which is usually focused on spiritual growth.

But this ministry did have one outreach event recently. They called it "Battle of the Bands." They drew out local rock bands for a night full of music and fun. They presented the gospel at the end of the night and had several students make decisions.

None of these programs, activities, or events are bad in any way. This ministry is just a little out of balance. They are stuck in the right column. No wonder this youth pastor doesn't know any *no-way* or even *not-interested kids*. None of them came to his *"Battle of the Bands."*

How is this ministry going to reach out to the community? All their eggs are in one outreach basket: "Battle of the Bands."

Maybe your ministry doesn't look like that at all. I've seen other churches with the opposite problem—they are stuck in the *"Outreach"* column. That ministry might look like this:

Outreach	Discipleship
Sunday Morning Discovery	Bible Studies
Wednesday Night Live	
Visit Local Campus	
Camp	
"Big Church"	
Cell Groups	

These ministries started emerging in the '90s as a polar reaction to the first example. This church wants to reach the community and focuses on outreach in almost everything. The problem is, there are not a lot of opportunities for spiritual growth.

As you can see, their left column is packed full. Sunday morning "Discovery" is their alternative to Sunday school. It's a time where they target unbelievers and present the gospel every week.

Wednesday Night Live does the same thing, but midweek.

This youth pastor is going on campus each week as well. It's here he meets many *not-interested kids* and even a few *no-way kids*. He actually got a few of them to go to his camp.

Cell groups for this church are small groups with an outreach focus. Each small group member is encouraged to bring friends, with the goal of doubling the size of the group. The small group material they use is examining key objections people have about God. The point is to provide answers to these objections and introduce people to Christ.

"Big Church" at this church also has an outreach focus. Each service targets unbelievers and gives an altar call or an opportunity to respond at the end.

Camp is also a huge outreach focus for this ministry. They try to draw as many students there as possible and present the gospel.

All of these are also great programs, activities, and ministry efforts—nothing wrong with any of them. But this ministry is also out of balance. With this much outreach going on, numerous students will be accepting Christ—but where do these students go to grow? I guess that's where this ministry's Bible study comes in—the lone item in their right column. The question is: Will that lone Bible study be enough? A believer attending this ministry will probably hear four gospel presentations a week and have just one place to focus on growing in faith. This ministry also seems way out of balance.

A BALANCED MINISTRY

Diverse students require diverse ministry methodology. In other words, if the church wants to reach out to our diverse population, its leaders might need to expand its ministry's focus or, at least, adjust the balance.

Sometimes we need to adjust our balance personally, too. On a personal level, are you involved in your local community so you can meet people in the outreach category?

My great aunt writes me each month. (Yes, an actual handwritten note sent in an envelope through the U.S. Postal Service—go figure.) This month she wrote something that really impressed me. My aunt loves her garden and her fruit trees. In the letter she told me how good her peach crop was doing this year. She wrote, "I have so many peaches this year—enough to bring to all my neighbors. It's a great way to get to know them all."

What a simple, basic way to build relationships with outreach neighbors. Peaches. Whodathunkit?

Some youth workers believe the job of the church is simply to cultivate Christian growth. If you're of this philosophy, I encourage you to look closely at Jesus' interactions with all types of people and at the early church in Acts. Ask yourself, How was the early church able to grow in number daily? The church should be reaching out to both *outreach* and *discipleship students*.

QUICK REVIEW:

Before we go on to STEP 7, let's review what we've accomplished so far to help us apply one-on-one to our ministry.

> STEP 1: You've recruited volunteer leaders who understand the priority of one-on-one relationships in your ministry. They understand you want to connect adults with students.

STEP 2: You've taught your leaders the difference be-tween outreach and discipleship ministry.

STEP 3: You've introduced the six types of students they will encounter.

STEP 4: You've inventoried your students—placing the names of students on a *six-types-of-students* table.

STEP 5: You've stood back and taken time to analyze your inventory, observing any trends or groupings on the chart, taking special note of groups of students you are missing.

STEP 6: You've made a separate chart to analyze your programming and ministry efforts. You checked your balance to identify if you favor outreach or discipleship. This might explain some of the reason you're missing certain types of students.

You've analyzed your ministry and taken the spiritual pulse of the students. You've probably even taken notice of areas where your ministry is weak. Now you have to ask yourself, *What are you going to do about it?*

STEP 7: Develop Individual Goals to Connect

Don't feel overwhelmed. All this analysis has probably revealed some areas of weakness. It may even require you to rethink some programming. But the main reason I use this tool is to make sure my leaders are connecting with all six types of students.

If you use this exercise, don't finish without setting relational goals. Help your entire ministry team develop a game plan for each of the students they will encounter.

For example, direct your team's attention back to individual sticky notes and ask them, "What should we do about Riley?"

Point to Riley's sticky note in the *checking-things-out* column. Ask the youth leader who wrote the note, "What are some of our goals with Riley?"

Discuss this as a group. Hopefully someone will come up with one of the most important needs that any student on the *outreach* side of the chart has—*she needs Christ.*

Others might point out some surface needs or felt needs. If no one seems to know Riley very well, then one of the biggest needs might be to get to know Riley better.

My objective as the leader of this team of adults is to make sure the adult leader in Riley's life has clear goals for Riley. I'd hope this leader would walk away from our training understanding:

- I want to get to know Riley better, becoming a good listener.

- I want Riley to know she has an adult who cares about her and is available for her.

- If Riley is indeed a *checking-things-out kid*, then I want to engage in spiritual conversations with Riley and share Christ with her.

Do this with each of the names on sticky notes. Make sure every adult leader has clear goals with each student. Brainstorm methods to transform students from left to right on the *six-types-of-students* table and make sure your leaders have a clear understanding of the process.

I like to follow up training like this with one-on-one time with each of my leaders (go figure). That way I can answer any individual questions they have and review the goals they set with each of their students.

Finally, be ready to provide resources for your adult leaders. Put books in their hands that will help them accomplish their goals. If they are working with *outreach students*, then you might want to give them a copy of my book *Do They Run When They See You Coming?* This is a book dedicated to helping youth leaders reach out to unchurched students without scaring them away.

AFTER THE SEVEN STEPS

After you are done training your staff, implement some accountability or occasional checkups that give you a chance to evaluate your efforts.

Meet Weekly to Share Progress

Each week we set aside time in our volunteer meetings for leaders to share stories of students' changed lives. This not only keeps us current with what's going on in the lives of the students we work with, it encourages our entire team.

Sometimes leaders can draw ideas from each other. "Wow! That was a great question you asked," or "Hiking? That's a good idea."

Weekly meetings foster a synergy in your team that motivates them to want to be a part of the impact that is taking place.

Track Changed Lives

Earlier in the chapter I shared that I like to use a big piece of butcher paper on my leadership retreats when I do that exercise with the *six-types-of-students* table and all the sticky notes. One reason I like it is I can then keep the information somewhere.

Some people might want to import their information onto some sort of spreadsheet. Others might like the simple paper with sticky notes. Regardless of your preference, I encourage you to keep a record of your initial "exercise" so you can refer back to it and track the changes in the lives of students in your group.

Track *outreach students* and see how many of them get to know Jesus. If they don't, then ask why not. Track *stagnant kids* and see how many of them move to the right on the table, becoming *growing kids*, and maybe eventually even *looking-for-ministry kids*.

It's exciting to see students moving to the right. It's sobering when students don't move at all. Keep track of this kind of life change.

Make It Easy for Your Leaders

Volunteer youth workers often live hectic lives, balancing work, school, family, etc. It's important for us to help them as much as we can, providing ideas of where and how to connect with students, as well as books and resources that provide direction.

Here are a few ideas I've used that were a help to my team. I've mentioned a few of them before, but they bear repeating:

- Purchase gift cards to local restaurants, coffee shops or ice cream parlors. Provide parameters of what the card should be used for (e.g., use every time you are with one of our students one-on-one. Turn in receipts with the name of the student you met with).

- Make specific goals for your leaders at camps or long trips. Make *one-on-one* time a goal (e.g., camp counselors meet with each one of their campers one-on-one at least once during the week).

- At camps and/or retreats, buy/create coupons to the snack bar so your leaders can buy students a soda or nachos during their time together.

- Provide your leaders with pocket money specifically for one-on-one time at camps or travel trips (ask them to give you receipts back with the names of the students they met with).

- Send your team emails with helpful articles or Web links that help them keep current with the students they are reaching (e.g., send them our ministry's weekly "Youth Culture Window" article).

- If you buy each person on your team Christmas gifts, why not buy them books or resources that help them minister to the students they are working with?

- Meet weekly as a group and share *one-on-one* experiences with each other.

Those are just a few examples that might be helpful for helping your leaders meet with students one-on-one.

All the Difference

Don't rush out and change your program.

Don't cancel Sunday school.

Don't switch your focus on Wednesday nights.

Don't fire your volunteers.

Sure, some adjustments might need to be made to all of those elements. I don't know. What I do know is I've seen hundreds of ministries with plenty of problems change one simple thing: They made one-on-one time with students a priority. Regardless of everything else, students were being invested in one student at a time, and that made all the difference in the world.

Try it. Start with the first *stagnant kid* in your group who comes to mind. You could begin with a simple text message. *"What's your favorite fast food? Ya wanna go there tomorrow after school?"*

What are you waiting for?

APPENDICES

APPENDIX A: SAMPLE STUDY
JESUS' ENCOUNTERS WITH PEOPLE

Scripture	Context	Audience	Action Taken	Message Communicated (if any)	Did he bring up "God stuff"
Matt. 3:13-17	Jesus is baptized.	People of Jerusalem, Judea, & the Jordan region	Jesus allows John the Baptist to baptize him.	Jesus replied, "Let it be so now; it is proper for us to do this to fulfill all righteousness." Then John consented. (v. 15, NIV)	Yes, I would consider referring to "the fulfillment of all righteousness" God stuff.
Matt. 4:1-11	Jesus is tempted by Satan.	Satan	Jesus used Scripture to defend against temptation.	I'm so much more than flesh and blood… I'm a spiritual being. No way.	Yes, he quoted Scripture, rebuking Satan.
Matt. 4:12-17	Jesus goes to Galilee, then Capernaum.	All the people "from that time on" (v.17).	Preaching	From that time on Jesus began to preach, "Repent, for the kingdom of heaven is near." (v.17, NIV)	Yes, he brought a message from God that said, "Turn from your own ways and turn to God."
Matt. 4:18-22	Jesus recruits his disciples.	Simon Peter, Andrew, James, and John	He asked them to follow him.	"Come, follow me," Jesus said, "and I will make you fishers of men." (v.19, NIV)	Yes, he basically asked them if they wanted to stop their temporary work to do "eternal" work.
Matt. 4:23, 25	Jesus teaches, preaches, and heals.	Large crowds from Galilee, the Decapolis, Jerusalem, Judea and the region across the Jordan followed him. (v. 25, NIV)	Jesus went throughout Galilee, teaching in their synagogues, preaching the good news of the kingdom, and healing every disease and sickness among the people. (v. 23, NIV)	Not mentioned	Yes, teaching in the synagogues and preaching the good news both convey "God stuff."
Matt. 4:24	Jesus heals.	Large crowds from Galilee, the Decapolis, Jerusalem, Judea and the region across the Jordan followed him. (v.25, NIV)	Jesus heals people.	Not mentioned	Not mentioned, although this verse is immediately after the verse that says Jesus was "teaching, preaching, and healing." So we don't know if these were three separate acts.

Scripture	Context	Audience	Action Taken	Message Communicated (if any)	Did he bring up "God stuff"
Matt. 5:1-7:29	Jesus gives the Sermon on the Mount.	His disciples (5:1) and the Jewish crowds (7:28).	He sat down to teach them.	The Beatitudes: Everything we need is from God, so be joyful while here on earth. The laws: Do unto others what you would have them do to you (7:12). Obedience and "fruit" are important.	Yes.
Matt. 8:1-4	Jesus heals the leper.	Large crowds following him after Sermon on the Mount	Heals leper and tells him to see a priest to become part of society again.	"Show yourself to the priest and offer the gift Moses commanded, as a testimony to them." (v.4, NIV)	Debatable; he did tell the man to do what the book of the law says, but it might have been simply so the man could become part of society again.
Matt. 8:5-13	Jesus heals the Roman centurion's servant.	Jesus had entered Capernaum (v. 5) and some people (unknown) were following him (v. 10).	He heals the centurion's servant from a distance just because of the man's faith.	"I tell you the truth, I have not found anyone in Israel with such great faith. I say to you that many will come from the east and the west, and will take their places at the feast with Abraham, Isaac and Jacob in the kingdom of heaven. But the subjects of the kingdom will be thrown outside, into the darkness, where there will be weeping and gnashing of teeth… Go! It will be done just as you believed it would." (vv.10-13, NIV)	Yes, he actually compares this Gentile's faith to many of the Jews' faith.
Matt. 8:14-15	Jesus heals Peter's mother-in-law.	In Peter's house after entering Capernaum	He healed her fever by touching her hand, and then she got up and began to wait on him.	Not mentioned	No.

Scripture	Context	Audience	Action Taken	Message Communicated (if any)	Did he bring up "God stuff"
Matt. 8:16-18	Jesus drives out spirits and heals the sick.	Many came after healing Peter's mother-in-law. The demon-possessed and sick were brought to him (v. 16) and crowds gathered (v. 18).	He drove out the spirits (demon-possessed) with a word and healed all the sick (v. 16).	With a "word" (word not mentioned…for all we know it could have been, "Leave," or, "Abracadabra!")	No, unless the word brought it up—like if the word was "repent."
Matt. 8:19-22	Some want to follow Jesus.	Perhaps the same crowds that had gathered when he healed the demon-possessed and the sick.	Not mentioned	Jesus tells the people who say they will follow him how hard it will be "foxes have holes" (v. 20) "…let the dead bury their own dead" (v. 22).	Yes.
Matt. 8:23-27	Jesus calms the storm.	The disciples in the boat.	Jesus rebuked the winds and the waves when the storm came up.	"You of little faith, why are you so afraid?" (v. 26)	Yes, he calls them people of little faith.
Matt. 8:28-34	Jesus sends the demons into pigs.	The disciples in the boat were there, the two demon-possessed men, those tending the pigs, and eventually "the whole town" (v.34) in the region of the Gadarenes. (Gentile town— hence the pigs.)	When the demons confronted him as the Son of God, they begged him to send them into the herd of pigs. Jesus did, and the pigs went kamikaze into the water.	Jesus said, "Go," (v.32).	No, unless you interpret his, "Go," as a confirmation of their claim that he was the Son of God coming to "torture them" before the appointed time.
Matt. 9:1-8	Jesus heals a paralytic brought to him on a mat.	His own town (v. 1), which was Capernaum. Teachers of the law were there (v. 3), and crowds (v. 8).	Jesus forgives the man's sins and heals him.	He says, "Take heart, son; your sins are forgiven," (v.2). Only after the teachers of the law confront him does he heal the man. He also claims to be the "Son of Man" (v.6).	Yes, clearly, he forgives him of his sins before healing him.

Scripture	Context	Audience	Action Taken	Message Communicated (if any)	Did he bring up "God stuff"
Matt. 9:9-13	Matthew follows Jesus and then invites him to dinner.	Mathew, disciples, notorious sinners, Pharisees observing this.	Jesus is hanging out with Matthew and his friends—all sinners. The Pharisees are critical of his company. Jesus corrects their judgment.	Jesus said, "It is not the healthy who need a doctor, but the sick. But go and learn what this means: 'I desire mercy, not sacrifice.' For I have not come to call the righteous, but sinners" (vv. 12-13).	Yes, he lets them know he came for those who are ready to admit their sin, not those who think they're already good enough. He even backs up his talk with Scripture, quoting Hosea 6:6, a passage where God was rebuking his people for their meaningless ritual with no "heart" behind it.

APPENDIX B:
THE SIX-TYPES-OF-STUDENTS CHART

Outreach			Discipleship		
No Way	Not Interested	Checking Things Out	Stagnant	Growing	Looking for Ministry

For more information about this chart, read chapter four of *Connect: Real Relationships in a World of Isolation* by Jonathan McKee, which provides a great overview of all six students with examples of what each looks like.

APPENDIX C:
QUESTIONS THAT HELP BREAK THE ICE

Here are some more examples of questions that might help you break the ice:

TV:

I'm doing a study on teenagers and the media. What do you think is the most popular TV show teenagers watch today?

Follow-up questions:

What is your favorite show?

What do you like about it?

Which character do you relate to the most? Why?

Which character do you relate to the least? Why?

What is your parents' favorite TV show?

What is one show you watch you don't want anyone else to know you watch?

What do you like about that show?

What would be embarrassing about others knowing you watch that show?

SPORTS:

Hey, you're wearing a LeBron jersey. Are you a Cavaliers fan or a LeBron fan?

Do you like watching basketball—or what is your favorite sport to watch?

What is your favorite sport to play?

ACTIVITIES:

What do you do with your leisure time? In other words, you've finished your homework and chores—now what?

What is your favorite activity to do on a typical Friday or Saturday night?

If you had your driver's license, where do you think you would drive most often?

NOTICING WHAT THEY ARE WEARING:

You've got Guitar Hero on your shirt. What system do you play it on?

Follow-up questions:

They say Guitar Hero is bringing back classic rock and roll. Are they right? Do you find yourself listening to some of the songs you play on the game?

What kind of music do you listen to most often?

Different Student:

You've got a Manchester United shirt on. Do you play soccer, or are you just a fan?

Follow-up questions:

Who's your favorite player?

What position do you play?

Do you see yourself still playing in five years?

SEASONAL:

(I might adjust these questions based on the group I'm talking to. If it was December, and they all celebrated Christmas, I'd change the vocabulary to *Christmas*. But I'd probably start with *holiday*, as not to exclude any students from other religions from the conversation.)

Who here has the most fun holiday plans?

What are they?

What part of these plans do you like the best?

Who here (to a group of students) has the worst holiday plans ever?

What are they?

What part of these plans do you hate the most?

Describe a typical religious holiday with your family.

Follow-up questions if they mention church as part of their plans: (Note: These are school-safe questions. In my area, I'd never bring up church on campus. But if they brought it up, I could ask the following questions without violating my agreement not to talk about God during school hours...)

Oh, what church are you going to?

Do you go there often, or just like Christmas, Easter?

Do you enjoy it?

What do you enjoy about it?

What do you not enjoy?

If you could change something about it, what would you change?

Notice many of these questions take a little bit of knowledge about pop culture and the media. Researching the attitudes and trends in culture actually pays off when you're standing among a circle of students, desperately trying to break the ice by asking questions.

APPENDIX D: REACT CARDS

MY REACTION

Name: _____

Phone: _____ (cell? home?)

☐ I enjoyed tonight's topic.

☐ I'd like to talk more about this...

☐ Why lie? I'd just like someone to take me to ice cream!

Comments: _____

_____

APPENDIX E:
VOLUNTEER EXPECTATIONS
YOUTH MINISTRY VOLUNTEER LEADERS

Our youth ministry has many opportunities available to help make a difference in students' lives. We have short-term project teams, set-up teams, and "help" roles—usually for people who can help only during certain hours of the week. But then we have a role we call our Volunteer Leaders—this page describes the expectations we have for those who can commit to spending weekly time with students.

Our volunteer leaders commit to investing in students regularly, in three different venues:

1. One-on-one times apart from youth group

2. Weekly youth group

3. Events and activities

One unique thing about being a youth ministry volunteer leader is the nature of the work we do. Encouraging, praying, and doing recreational activities with students is exciting. At the end of a rough day or week, this ministry isn't another pressure or loathed time commitment; it is a time for which one can set all else aside and allow God to work through him or her doing something enjoyable.

ONE-ON-ONE TIMES WITH STUDENTS

Spending one-on-one time with students is the most important thing we do. These students are seeking attention and guidance. They all want to be listened to, noticed, and appreciated. Some of these students don't get much individual attention at home. Some don't know what it is to be liked, heard, or cared about. We can help fill that void in their lives.

Each staff person needs to be in contact with students weekly. Sometimes this might just be a phone call or a "text" to see how things are going or if they are coming to the next event. At least once a month, volunteer leaders need to meet with a student outside of ministry events and activities. My hope is leaders could meet more frequently than once a month—weekly or every other week would be ideal. These meetings include any activity with just one (sometimes two) student(s). Volunteer leaders can take students out for a milkshake, go shopping with them, stand in line at the DMV with them—you can go almost anywhere. Some students who drive you nuts during youth group are wonderful one-on-one because they respond completely differently when away from friends.

WEDNESDAY NIGHTS

In order to better accommodate busy schedules, our volunteer leader meetings and youth group programs will be on the same nights. Occasionally, volunteer leaders will also meet on Sunday night for dinner, fun times of fellowship and planning.

Youth group is from 7:00-8:30 every Wednesday evening. It is an important time to get to know students in our church and invite other students whom you've met in the community.

SPECIAL ACTIVITIES

Trips to Disneyland, monthly events, ski retreats, camping, etc., are not only free to volunteer leaders, but are also invaluable opportunities to spend extended time with students.

ENDNOTES

[i] Clark, Chap. *Hurt: Inside the World of Today's Teenagers*. Grand Rapids, MI: Baker Publishing Group, 2004.

[ii] Pelt, Rich Van, and Jim Hancock. *The Youth Worker's Guide to Helping Teenagers in Crisis*. Zondervan, 2008.

[iii] Baden, Evan. *A Collection of Unexpected Photography; The Illuminati*. http://www.filemagazine.com/galleries/archives/2008/04/the_illuminati.html.

[iv] McPherson, Miller, Lynn Smith-Lovin, and Matthew E. Brashears. "Social Isolation in America: Changes in Core Discussion Networks over Two Decades." *American Sociological Review* 71 (2006). http://www.asanet.org/galleries/default-file/June06ASRFeature.pdf.

[v] "ItsJustLunch Advertisement." *Hemispheres Magazine*. United Airlines, June 2008. 77.

[vi] Vertis Communications. "'Decade of Data' Study Reveals Key Trends." Marketing Charts. January 17, 08. http://www.marketingcharts.com/television/decade-of-data-study-reveals-key-trends-3084/.

[vii] Goodstein, Anastasia. "Remotely Connected." PBS.org. January 13, 2008. http://www.pbs.org/remotelyconnected/2008/01/frontline_growing_up_online.html.

[viii] Smith, David R. "Youth Culture Window; The Hottest Virtual Teenage Hangout...A Little Too 'Hot'." thesource4ym.com. http://www.thesource4ym.com/YouthCultureWindow/article.asp?ID=41.

[ix] Dye, Lee. *Teens Prefer Computers to Doctors*. June 4, 2008. http://www.abcnews.go.com/Technology/GadgetGuide/Story?id=4989614&page=1.

[x] McKee, Jonathan. *Getting Students to Show Up*. Zondervan, 2007: 23.

[xi] Pew Forum on Religion and Public Life. http://religions.pewforum.org/pdf/report-religious-landscape-study-full.pdf.

[xii] Kimball, Dan. *They Like Jesus, But Not the Church*. Zondervan, 2007.

[xiii] Barna. *Beliefs: General Religious*. http://www.barna.org/FlexPage.aspx?Page=Topic&TopicID=2.

[xiv] Strobel, Lee. *Inside the Mind of Unchurched Harry and Mary*. Zondervan, 1993.

[xv] Grossman, Cathy Lynn. "Survey: More have dropped dogma for spirituality in U.S. ." *USA Today*. June 23, 2008. http://www.usatoday.com/news/religion/2008-06-23-pew-religions_N.htm.

[xvi] *Time*. August 6, 2007: 6.

[xvii] *Jane*. March 2005: 109.

[xviii] Kimball, Dan. *They Like Jesus, But Not the Church*. Zondervan, 2007.

[xix] McKee, Jonathan. *Do They Run When They See You Coming?:Reaching Out to Unchurched Teenagers*. Zondervan, 2005.

[xx] "Hayden Panettiere, Interview." www.thesource4ym.com. October 19, 2004.

[xxi] Stier, Greg. *Dare 2 Share: A Field Guide to Sharing Your Faith*. Focus on the Family, 2006.

[xxii] McKee, Jonathan. *Do They Run When They See You Coming?: Reaching Out to Unchurched Teenagers*. Zondervan, 2005.

[xxiii] "The Barna Update; Fewer Than 1 in 10 Teenagers Believe that Music Piracy is Morally Wrong." Barna.org. April 26, 2004. http://www.barna.org/FlexPage.aspx?Page=BarnaUpdate&BarnaUpdateID=162.

[xxiv] Smith, David R. "Youth Culture Window." thesource4ym.com. http://www.thesource4ym.com/YouthCultureWindow/article.asp?ID=41.

[xxv] Simon, Mallory. "Online Student-Teacher Friendships Can Be Tricky." CNN.com. August 12, 2008. http://www.cnn.com/2008/TECH/08/12/studentsteachers.online/.

[xxvi] Burns, Jim, and Mike Devries. *Partnering With Parents in Youth Ministry* . Regal Books, 2003.

[xxvii] Devries, Mark. *Family-Based Youth Ministry: Reaching the Been-There, Done-That Generation*. InterVarsity Press, 1994.

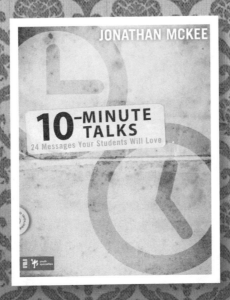

If you need to communicate something meaningful in just a little time, *10-Minute Talks* has just what you need—more than two dozen ready-to-go, story-based talks. With talks for spiritual growth, targeted at your Christian students, and outreach talks, perfect for any teenager, you'll be prepared to give them a bite of truth that they can walk away remembering. You'll say less, but communicate more!

10-Minute Talks
24 Messages Your Students Will Love

Jonathan McKee
Retail $24.99
978-0-310-27494-0

Visit www.youthspecialties.com
or your local bookstore.

Getting Students to Show Up will challenge you to re-think your methodology when it comes to outreach. But more than that, it'll show you, step-by-step, how to plan and execute a great outreach event for 10 or even 10,000 students.

Whether you're going for a city-wide shindig or a weekly gathering for your church or a campus, you'll find plenty of tips and tools inside that will ensure your event actually reaches out to your demographic and points them toward Jesus.

Getting Students to Show Up
Practical Ideas for Any Outreach Event—from 10 to 10,000

Jonathan McKee
Retail $12.99
978-0-310-27216-8

Visit www.youthspecialties.com
or your local bookstore.

Open your doors to students outside the church! Full of real-life examples, the insights of this book will inspire you to see students as Jesus sees them—with grace and compassion. The unchurched can be reached, but it starts with knowing what you're doing, and doing it with love.

Do They Run When They See You Coming?
Reaching Out to Unchurched Teenagers

Jonathan McKee
Retail $12.99
978-0-310-25660-1

Visit www.youthspecialties.com
or your local bookstore.